THE FOUR-WEEK CYCLE OF PSALMS AND CANTICLES ARRANGED FOR

MORNING AND EVENING PRAYER AND INCLUDING PSALMS FOR

MIDDAY AND NIGHT PRAYER IN A STUDY TRANSLATION

PREPARED BY THE INTERNATIONAL COMMISSION ON

ENGLISH IN THE LITURGY.

S0-AHM-499

PSALMS

for Morning and Evening Prayer

 LITURGY TRAINING PUBLICATIONS

IMPRIMATUR

In accord with canon 825, §1 of the Code of Canon Law, the National Conference of Catholic Bishops hereby approves for publication the *Liturgical Psalter,* a translation of the Psalms submitted by the International Commission on English in the Liturgy.

William Cardinal Keeler, D.D., J.C.D.
President, National Conference of Catholic Bishops
Washington, DC, January 5, 1995.

ACKNOWLEDGMENTS

The English translation of the psalms and canticles is from *The Liturgical Psalter: Text for Study and Comment,* © 1994 by the International Committee on English in the Liturgy, Inc. (ICEL); the English translation of the antiphons and the music for the psalm tones and antiphons are from *Daily Praise: A Study of Morning, Evening, and Night Prayer,* © 1995, ICEL. All rights reserved. For reprint permission, write: ICEL, 1522 K Street NW, Suite 1000, Washington DC 20005-1202.

"An Introduction to the Translation" by Mary Collins, OSB, reprinted from *Worship* (July 1992) with permission.

Art: Linda Ekstrom. Design: Kerry Perlmutter.
Editor: Gabe Huck. Editorial assistant: Jennifer McGeary.

Library of Congress Cataloging-in-Publication Data
International Committee on English in the Liturgy.
    Psalms for morning and evening prayer / [art, Linda Ekstrom].
        p. 336
    1. Psalters. 2. Catholic Church—Prayer-books and devotions—English. 3. Catholic Church—Liturgy. 4. Bible. O.T. Psalms—Devotional use. I. Ekstrom, Linda. II. Bible. O.T. English. 1994. III. Title.
BX2033.C38 1994
264′ .028—dc20   93-29349
                                                                    CIP

ISBN 0-929650-76-X (casebound)   C/MEP
ISBN 0-929650-89-1 (paperbound)   P/MEP

Copyright © 1995, Archdiocese of Chicago: Liturgy Training Publications, 1800 North Hermitage Avenue, Chicago IL 60622-1101. All rights reserved.

For additional copies or more information: 1-800-933-1800; FAX 1-800-933-7094.

CONTENTS

The International Commission on English in the Liturgy (ICEL) acknowledges with gratitude the editorial committee and the subcommittee and its consultants who have ably and generously assisted at various stages of this project. It should be noted that some of the subcommittee members served for as many as 14 years. ICEL also thanks those parishes, religious communities, liturgical commissions and individuals who sent comments as the work progressed.

EDITORIAL COMMITTEE

Lawrence Boadt, CSP
Mary Collins, OSB
John Dzieglewicz, SJ
Peter Finn
Joseph Wimmer, OSA

SUBCOMMITTEE MEMBERS AND CONSULTANTS

Peter Barry
Lawrence Boadt, CSP
Rita Burns
Daniel Coughlin
Mary Collins, OSB
Margaret Daly
John Dzieglewicz, SJ
Peter Finn
Leslie Hoppe, OFM
Roderick MacKenzie, SJ
Mary McGann, RSCJ
John McGuckin
Marjorie Moffatt, SNJM

Joseph Mulrooney
Irene Nowell, OSB
James Schellman
Eileen Schuller, OSU
Geoffrey Boulton Smith
Pamela Stotter
Carroll Stuhlmueller, CP
Michael Suarez, SJ
Francis Sullivan, SJ
Thomas Troeger
Elizabeth-Anne Vanek
Christopher Willcock, SJ
Joseph Wimmer, OSA

FOREWORD

The first words—in time, in importance—are the words that are handed on to us, are received and repeated until they belong to us, then are handed on once more. Thus have the psalms been the first words of Jews and of Christians. They are our prayers and our teacher of prayer. They are our vocabulary, the language we speak.

Morning and evening, the day's hinges that have always brought people to their brief or lengthy rituals, are for us the time to pray in psalms. The words for morning, the words for evening, join individual Christians and households and communities. We become the church praying. Thus do we praise when praise is due, even when it comes hard. Thus do we lament, intercede, give thanks. With these words of the psalms we put on the Lord Jesus Christ and make the day ahead or the night ahead into moments of God's reign.

Our time has seen many attempts to translate the psalms into an English that has the strength and beauty to bear repetition, for it is only such repetition that can transform the one who prays. The translation in this book was prepared under the direction of the International Commission on English in the Liturgy. Poets, musicians, Hebrew and biblical scholars were involved in each text. Their charter was to prepare a translation for public prayer, a text that would be worthy contemporary poetry and contemporary expression. One hope is that the use of these texts will stimulate various reactions which can, in turn, lead to an evaluation before this translation is proposed as an approved English version for the liturgy. Those who use this book are invited to offer their general or specific comments to the International Commission on English in the Liturgy at the address found on the acknowledgment page.

This book orders the psalms and canticles through a four-week cycle of Morning and Evening Prayer. The order is that found in the Liturgy of the Hours. Many psalms for Midday Prayer and Night Prayer are also provided. The various introductions that begin this book will be of great help whether one is newly come to the psalms or has lived with them for years.

Often those who have placed the words of the psalms on paper have done so with great care: that the beauty of the letters themselves, the beauty of the page and of the book, might mirror the beauty and strength of the psalms. This book wishes to stand in that tradition. It recognizes that the psalms are first and last not words on a page but words in the mouth of a Jew or a Christian, words spoken and words chanted. Printed word and accompanying art are but an effort to hear that chanting and allow one more person to join in. In this spirit, the book was designed by Kerry Perlmutter with attention in every detail to the dignity of its content and the requirements for its use.

The artist, Linda Ekstrom, worked to make art that would both listen to and dialogue with the text. It is as filled as the words themselves with possible meanings, with the varieties of human experience and mood. Both psalms and images return in their due cycle of weeks, each new meeting echoing and mirroring the previous times, each new meeting departing from all other times.

The publisher's great thanks go to all who had some part in fashioning this book: the staff of the International Commission on English in the Liturgy, the translators and review committees, the designer and the artist, and those who offered counsel on the book's contents and presentation as it took shape during 1992 (especially Andrew Ciferni, Mary Collins, Mary McGann, Irene Nowell and Frank Quinn). May we all remember one another in the church's prayer.

Gabe Huck

An Introduction to
THE BOOK OF PSALMS

O pening the Book of Psalms is like walking into a home, lived in for many generations. Photos and mementos, some ancient and some new, blend together. Some are well preserved, others were dropped and cracked by the children, still others have faded, and a few are even difficult to identify. Only the grandparents know the story of each precious remembrance—if only they were still with us.

We turn to our ancestors in the faith to hear what they tell us about this sacred home, their house of prayer, the Book of Psalms. As in the family homestead, some psalms are carefully preserved, like Psalm 70, and others are almost indecipherable, like Psalms 2:11–12 and 141:5–7. Still others, like Psalm 139, use rare Hebrew forms, possibly some Aramaic words or endings. Yet whatever be the problem, this psalm is so well loved. Another section of psalms, sometimes called the curse or vindictive psalms, for instance Psalm 69:23–29, may be translated confidently enough, but their angry outbursts against the enemy embarrass Jews and Christians alike and have been dropped from the liturgical prayer of most churches. The family home unfortunately still harbors its grudges and feuds. The psalms, like the home, lead us through many stages of life, necessary to carry on, even if not our finest moments.

The psalms remained so precious that the early Christians never added their own book of prayer to the New Testament. They stayed at home with the prayer book of their religious ancestors.

FROM OBEDIENCE TO EXULTATION

In paging through our Bible we notice that this house of prayer or Book of Psalms is divided into five rooms or sections. Each of the first four rooms, or "books" as they are called, ends with a doxology of praise, differing only in the degree of excitement:

> *Blessed be the Lord,*
> *God of Israel for ever.*
> *Amen! Amen! (41:14)*

> *Blessed be Israel's God,*
> *Lord of wonderful deeds!*
> *Bless God's name for ever!*
> *Let God's glory fill the world!*
> *Amen and Amen! (72:18-19)*

> *Blessed be God for ever. Amen. Amen. (89:53)*

> *Blessed is the Lord,*
> *the God of Israel,*
> *from eternity to eternity.*
> *Let all the people sing*
> *"Amen! Hallelujah!" (106:48)*

The first book begins with a reflection upon the law, the happy and fruitful life of the obedient person, "like a tree planted by a stream, . . . its yield always plenty," and the dismal, barren life of the wicked, "like chaff . . . blown by the wind." The fifth book concludes with Psalm 150 and its thunderous roll of hallelujahs. Thirteen variations of this Hebrew word summon every person to "praise God." The five books of psalms continuously reach to the heavens ecstatic with wonder. Whatever be the circumstances of sorrow and death, puzzlement and questioning, gratitude and confidence, joy and excitement, even anger and feelings of revenge, within the five rooms or books of psalms, each day or moment asks for obedience to God and ends with its Amen! Hallelujah! praising God.

THE FIVE ROOMS OF ISRAEL'S HOUSE OF PRAYER

As happens when children are born within a family, Israel was adding new rooms or "books" to its home. Each new generation faced new life situations. In many ways each of the five books holds a mirror to the age when an editor gathered its psalms together and responded to life's realities.

Dark clouds hang over the *first book* (Psalms 1–41) with a heavy presence of lament and supplication. Praise, as in Psalms 8, 19 or 29, at times interrupts the dismal landscape. Yet the majority of these psalms reflects depression days. They accompany the tears and groans of individual Jewish people after their return to a devastated homeland around 537 BCE. Despite it all, the first book ends with its Amen, its strong affirmation of faith in God's presence through it all.

Later, after the rebuilding of the Temple and its dedication in 515 BCE, another scribe, from a guild of writers under the patronage of Korah, adds a new collection of psalms. These focus on worship in the Jerusalem Temple and become the *second book*, Psalms 42–72. The signature of Korah is delicacy, longing and joyful memories of worship:

> *As a deer craves running water,*
> *I thirst for you, my God . . .*
> *I cry my heart out,*
> *I remember better days. (42:2, 5)*

The *third book* (Psalms 73–89) opens with songs, strong and confident, realistic and responsive, from a different group of writers under the name of Asaph. They seem to echo the time of the great religious reforms of Ezra around 428 BCE (see Ezra, chapter 10, and Nehemiah, chapters 8–9 and 13).

As will happen with any home, the family adds other things—a ramp for a sick or elderly person, some toys for a child, and mementos from an anniversary celebration. The *fourth book* (Psalms 90–106) collects these stray pieces.

Finally the *fifth and final book* (Psalms 107–150) contains psalms for pilgrimage to Jerusalem (Psalms 120–134), others for singing at the three great pilgrimage festivals (Psalms 113–118). Perhaps we can place this collection after the conquests and new world order of Alexander the Great, sometime around 300 BCE.

The psalms, therefore, appear as a liturgical or prayerful response to the needs of each new age of Israel's history. The scribes or editors assembled and wrote down these hymns and prayers within a book of psalms, not in any chronological order of composition but pastorally as the people needed them.

Some of this explanation depends upon the "titles" of the psalms, omitted in our liturgy but printed in our Bibles at the beginning of most of the psalms. Other aspects derive from our effort to coordinate the dominant attitude within each book of psalms with important moments in the history of Israel after the Babylonian exile.

THE WEAR AND TEAR OF USE

New generations will do more than add rooms. They shift furniture around and give old pieces new uses. A careful reading shows that the biblical Book of Psalms demonstrates the wear and tear of long use in the temple, synagogue and home. Psalm 14 repeats itself as Psalm 53; Psalm 70 appears within 40:14–18. The differences almost slip by unnoticed. While Psalms 14 and 40 address God by the divine name, Psalms 53 and 70 try to avoid that most sacred word, whose Hebrew form was never spoken in postexilic Israel except once a year by the High Priest on the feast of Yom Kippur, the Day of Atonement. In fact, "Lord" almost never occurs within one series of psalms, 42–53.

We have no certain explanation for this change from "Lord" to "God," except to suggest that the title "Lord" was too sacred for daily prayer and so its easy use struck people as offensive or blasphemous. This change in biblical times might support other changes within modern translations of the psalms. Some versions, like the one within this book, avoid words that are offensive or give a wrong meaning, like the word "men" when we really mean "women and men." The ancient Bible, especially the psalms, was primarily a liturgical text and lived within the changing circumstances of people's lives.

Still other adaptations occurred as Jewish people prayed the psalms. They composed a new Psalm 108 out of sections from two earlier psalms. How this new composition came into existence gives an excellent example of adapting earlier inspired psalms to a new situation.

Psalm 57 lays bare the fears of a timid person, hounded by people whose "teeth [are] like spears and arrows, [whose] tongues [are] sharp as swords" (verse 5). God rewards such humble patience, and the psalmist wakes the dawn to sing with harp and lyre (verse 9). Psalm 60, on the contrary, shouts defiance at the enemy and then calls upon God to "stretch out your hand, rescue us," you who "shook the land" until it "shuddered and split." In deleting parts of each psalm and combining other sections, the new Psalm 108 modifies the fierceness of Psalm 60 and strengthens the timidity of Psalm 57.

There are times today when some biblical texts and psalms are either too strident and confident, or else too weak and indecisive. We need to follow the lead of our ancestors by adapting the text, blending passages and so reaching a new inspired message.

These matters may seem trivial, yet sometimes the character of a person or of a family home shows up in attention to small, delicate details, adapting to guests and to unexpected turns of events.

Yet changes were not made on a whim. The scribes carefully guarded the text of the psalms. By counting every letter and verse, they could determine the middle letter and the middle verse of the entire psalter. The middle letter turned out to be *ayin* within the phrase "wild boars," literally "beasts from the forest," in Psalm 80:14. This letter they elevate and so highlight in every Hebrew Bible. *Ayin* is not only a letter of the alphabet but is also the word for "eye" and "spring." Each flows with water or tears. The meaning can be: At the center of the entire psalter, the eye of God looks upon us at every moment, at times even to drop a tear of compassion.

This spirit of divine compassion is again clear in the middle *verse* of all 150 psalms:

> *Yet God, in compassion,*
> *did not destroy them,*
> *but held back anger,*
> *restrained fury,*
> *forgave their sin. (78:38)*

Wear and tear bring tears of suffering and of joy, but most of all they deepen our compassion and enable our hearts to forgive as God does.

FROM PRAISE AND DESOLATION
TO THANKSGIVING AND WISDOM

Up until now we have examined the Book (or Five Books) of Psalms as found in our Bible. The format shows a sensitivity to the changing pastoral needs of ancient Israel and directs us likewise to be sensitive to the religious and social expectations of our day and age. We turn to individual types of prayers within the psalms.

Some of the most ancient psalms are *hymns of praise*. Numbered among these are Psalms 8, 19, 29 and 104. These hymns of praise hardly, if ever, speak of sin or sorrow. Rather, with their good eye they see a presence of God that is wondrous, overwhelming and most pure. They perceive the world and humankind as good and beautiful, fresh from the creative, caring hand of God:

> *Lord our God,*
> *the whole world tells*
> *the greatness of your name.*
> *Your glory reaches*
> *beyond the stars . . .*
> *What is humankind*
> *that you remember them,*
> *the human race*
> *that you care for them?*
> *You treat them like gods,*
> *dressing them in glory and splendor. (8:2, 5−6)*

These hymns draw their motivation not just from God's marvelous universe but also from God's magnificent care for Israel, especially in the wilderness during the days of Moses and Miriam. Psalm 114 is the song of passover exultation:

> *Israel marches out of Egypt . . .*
> *The sea pulls back for them,*
> *the Jordan flees in retreat.*
> *Mountains jump like rams,*
> *hills like lambs in fear . . .*
> *Why shudder, mountains, like rams?*
> *Why quiver, hills, like lambs?*
> *Tremble! earth, before the Lord,*
> *before the God of Jacob,*
> *who turns rock to water,*
> *flint to gushing streams. (114:1, 3−4, 6−8)*

Such hymns of praise rebound triumphantly from the majestic walls of Jerusalem's Temple. Other hymns acclaim this home of Israel's fearful yet compassionate, distant yet ever present God:

> *Holy mountain, beautiful height,*
> *crown of the earth!*
> *Zion, highest of sacred peaks,*
> *city of the Great King!*
> *God enthroned in its palaces*
> *becomes our sure defense! (48:2–4)*

Another series of early psalms provides a ritual for the enthronement of a king as well as for royal marriages and regal festivals (Psalms 2, 45, 72, 110), or as in Psalm 89, they add a prayer of supplication after a serious defeat.

Psalms of sorrow and supplication, as already mentioned, occupy major space in the first book of the psalter (Psalms 1–41). Yet these were written later than many of the hymns and show the strong influence of the prophets, especially Jeremiah, who repeatedly questioned and argued against God (see Jeremiah 12:1–5; 20:7–18). The clearest quality of this new set of psalms is honesty, even to the point of testing the limits of orthodoxy.

> *God, my God,*
> *why have you abandoned me—*
> *far from my cry, my words of pain?*
> *I call by day, you do not answer;*
> *I call by night, but find no rest. (22:1–2)*

In this psalm a person's question to God, now a part of the Bible, becomes the inspired word of God and paradoxically God's answer to the questioner. God's word is not always in crystal statements of truth. Rather, God appears within the human process of struggling without finding, of being left only with a question, bleakly and darkly in Psalm 88. The psalms embrace an absent God, mystically present in our questions.

The prayers of supplication sometimes speak in the singular, as in Psalm 22; others, voicing the community's pain and desolation, speak in the plural, as in Psalm 44. This psalm begins with an energetic statement of faith in the ancestral traditions (verses 2–9), then proceeds at once to contradict itself:

> *You, God, rescued us from danger*
> *and put our foes to shame . . .*
> *You force us to retreat*
> *while the enemy plunders our goods . . .*
> *I turn red with shame*
> *when I hear cruel taunts*
> *from foes wanting revenge. (44:8, 11, 16–17)*

The psalm is audacious enough—or is it better to say, honest enough?—to fling the gauntlet before the deity:

> *Wake up! Why do you sleep, Lord? (44:24)*

and so contradicts another psalm which quietly and confidently addresses "the guardian of Israel [who] neither rests nor sleeps" (Psalm 121:4). Desperately Psalm 44 plunges beyond the limits of orthodoxy, not to deny the truth but to declare that some human experiences defy all rational explanation, even that of good theologians and inspired biblical authors.

Another group of psalms, of *thanksgiving* and *confidence*, usher up front what remains only a conclusion in other psalms. Only Psalm 88 remains dark and abandoned throughout. Psalm 118 first thanks God for personal favors and then joins these with the gratitude of all Israel. Psalm 16, despite ridicule and shame heaped upon the devout Israelite, expresses a staunch, humble loyalty to God:

> *Lord, you measure out my portion,*
> *the shape of my future;*
> *you mark off the best place for me. (16:5–6)*

While most of the preceding psalms spring into life from heroic moments, whether of overwhelming joy and ecstatic wonder or of deadening desolation and shameful rejection, there are still other psalms for the moderate, normal everydays of life. It is ordinarily true, as Psalm 1 states:

> *The Lord marks the way of the upright,*
> *but the corrupt walk to ruin. (1:6)*

This golden rule of moderation and trust is put as plainly as possible in another *psalm of the wisdom tradition*:

> *From my youth to my old age*
> *never have I seen the just cast off*
> *or their children begging bread. (37:25)*

Yet even the wisdom tradition was tested beyond its resources of correct and just retribution on earth, so that the psalmists sometimes rushed on where angels stand in fear. Wisdom psalms that seem the most down to earth, practical to the point of being pragmatic, reach the limits of earthly reward and punishment and momentarily peer into a life beyond this life. The language is not as clear as the theologian would like it to be, but it smacks of the honesty and hesitation that seem to stalk our thoughts of heaven as we pick our way over sticky quagmires of distress:

> *You teach me wisdom,*
> *leading me to glory.*
> *What more would I have in heaven?*
> *Who else delights me on earth?*
> *If mind and body fail,*
> *you, God, are my rock,*
> *my support for ever. (73:24–26)*

The longest psalm of all plods slowly, surely, faithfully over the way of each person's life, submitting each step to God's help and guidance. Psalm 119 leaves no stage of our existence without God's strong protection.

CONCLUSION

The psalms bring us home to God, no matter how we are dressed, how we feel, what we have done or left undone. What they ask is already present in our heart from the opening Psalm 1, the gift of faith in God's loving presence, to Psalm 150 with its chorus of hallelujahs. The psalms lead us through the sections or rooms of our life, always ending with a strong Amen. Walking along, we are never alone but in the company of our saintly ancestors. When our questions arise, as happened to the two persons on their way to Emmaus, Jesus appears to declare that "everything written about me in the law of Moses and in the prophets and *psalms* must be fulfilled" (Luke 24:44). Through the psalms Jesus opens our mind to the hidden mysteries within our lives.

Carroll Stuhlmueller, CP

An Introduction to
THE LITURGY OF THE HOURS

T he people of God are pilgrims in time. We are perhaps most aware of living the ordinary rhythms dictated by the school calendar, the fiscal year, project time lines, civic commemorations, personal and family events and anniversaries. We study the past, immerse ourselves in the present, plan for the future, all within the inevitable horizon of human mortality.

At the same time, however, we live by another calendar of which we are often less conscious. As persons baptized into Jesus Christ, we have died and risen with Christ into a different history. It is the history of the new humanity created in Christ through the mystery of the cross. We are the body of Christ. We follow Christ through death into life beyond any measure of time as we have known it. Our time is paschal time; our history is paschal history. We live its hidden rhythms in every day's small deaths to the unredeemed way of being which is the heritage of sin, and every day's small risings to a way of life defined by the gospel law of love for God and neighbor.

Generations of Christians have woven a tradition of praying at significant moments of the day in order to live a life dictated by our deepest reality, the reality of a humanity redeemed in Jesus Christ and committed to the exodus journey that leads to the promised reign of God. Ours is a prayer of remembrance: We tell again and again the story of God's great deeds on our behalf, lest we forget who God is and who we are, and wander off. It is a prayer of thanksgiving: We begin here the song of praise that will be ours to sing forever at journey's end in the new Jerusalem. It is a prayer of petition for ourselves and for others: We lay our needs in trust before the God who has been faithful to us all along the way, for we are uncertain travelers, and the road before us is long. Christian tradition invites us to stop at certain times along the daily way to remember, to give thanks and to make petition, so that by praying at fixed times we may learn to pray at all times to God.

THE TIMES

The cycles of light and darkness, sun and moon, have controlled the pattern of the human journey through millennia and across continents. The first Christians built upon Jewish tradition to create a daily pattern of prayer at sunset and sunrise, at noon and at night, and later at other natural breaks in the day, counted as the third, sixth and ninth hours. Among those hours, sunset and sunrise have always had a special importance as the two "hinges" of the day.

Each hour of prayer has acquired certain characteristic themes. The light of the rising sun reveals the colors of a landscape made monochrome by night; it evokes the sounds of city and countryside stirring into life; it brings to life all that seemed somehow dead, though only quiet in sleep. Even for those who work or play by night in an electrified world, life takes on a different quality when daylight comes. Christian tradition has seen in the dawn a vivid image of the rising of the Sun of Justice, Jesus Christ, to usher in the eternal day of the new Jerusalem. Texts expressing praise for morning, light, creation and Christ's coming on the day of glory have seemed especially suitable for morning use. But the hours of our paschal history are made up of moments both dark and light. The return of wakefulness is for many a return of pain. Lament psalms, too, find their place in the church's morning prayer, for whether we are glad or sorry to see the new day come, we fix its beginning in prayer. And even the lament psalms end in hope, for every day holds the promise of that great and final day when our road will carry us into the unquenchable light of the city of God.

At evening, the descent of darkness hints at death, but in the paradox of paschal time, death is the moment of birth.

Evening prayer once marked the beginning rather than the end of the liturgical day. It still signals the beginning of Sundays and solemnities. The texts traditional for evening invite us to look back and forward. We look back to give thanks for the day behind us, and we look forward to welcome, beyond the seemingly impenetrable veil of sleep and death, the morning's promised light, Christ, the light no darkness can extinguish.

Additional night and day hours round out the cycle of daily prayer handed on to us by our tradition. Night prayer, which brings the day to a close, brings repentance for our failures to keep the morning's promise and confidence in the triumph of the light over sin and death. Midday prayer offers the opportunity to stop for prayer at noon, or at any other moment of the working day, to recall the road we travel in the ordinary round of daily activities. (The texts that were customary for the vigil service, now known as the Office of Readings and modified for use at any hour, do not appear in this book.)

THE PSALMS

Remembrance, thanksgiving and petition are intertwined in the psalms, which Christians over the centuries have made the core of this tradition of praying at certain times of the day. In these texts, every mood of the human heart is brought before God in praise and complaint, in trust and in anguished question, in hope and bewilderment, but always in prayer.

In our age of high technology, praying these poems sung in ancient Israel requires a certain effort. Where they are simple and direct expressions of universal human experience, they require no more than our fidelity. As we repeat the unfamiliar words over and over, day by day, until they become familiar, we discover gradually that the song they are singing is indeed our own. However, where they seem difficult to grasp, we may find that we can follow them more effectively if we recognize them as a doorway into the larger world of biblical literature. When we accept their invitation to enter into that world and to learn the great stories to which they allude — stories of creation and exodus, of political plots and the doings of kings and queens, of exile and return — we may find them far clearer than they at first appeared.

The psalms in this book are accompanied by antiphons. These may simply highlight some image or theme from the text, or they may juxtapose the psalm to the mystery of Christ. An antiphon is a short refrain that may be prayed before the psalm, or repeated between the verses in the style of a responsorial psalm, or said both before and afterward.

The psalms repay the fidelity of those who pray them regularly. Like Jacob after his night of wrestling with the angel, we may come away from our efforts to penetrate their different levels of meaning wounded by the word's sharp edges, but we also come away carrying the remedy. As the day unfolds, we begin to find that lines and phrases float up from memory to light the path before us, or simply to recall us into the presence of God even in the most unlikely situations.

Contemporary readers must not be limited by modern conveniences such as book titles. Although the 150 songs to which we commonly give the name of "psalm" are found in the Book of Psalms, they are not the only texts deserving of the name. Other poems, similar in structure, content or style, are scattered throughout the other books of the Jewish and Christian scriptures. They, too, have found their way into the Christian tradition of prayer. However, to distinguish them, custom calls them "canticles" rather than "psalms." The word itself reminds us that both psalms and canticles are poetry intended to be sung.

A canticle from the Jewish scriptures always appears between the first and second psalms of Morning Prayer; a canticle from the New Testament always appears as the final "psalm" of Evening Prayer. Three canticles from Luke's gospel also have their place in the hours. The Canticle of Zechariah (Luke 1:68–79), often called by the first word of the Latin text, "Benedictus," is customarily used at Morning Prayer; the Canticle of Mary (Luke 1:46–55), known as the "Magnificat," appears in Evening Prayer; and the Canticle of Simeon (Luke 2:29–32), the "Nunc Dimittis," is recited at Night Prayer.

In order to allow us to pray a large portion of the psalter and other scripture books, the psalms and canticles appointed for morning and evening recur in a four-week cycle. This book follows the cycle found in the *Liturgy of the Hours*. The psalms chosen for midday and night, being shorter and fewer in number, are repeated more frequently. The reader may select any midday or night psalm from the appropriate sections of the book.

The *Liturgy of the Hours* offers special selections for the major celebrations of the church year. An individual or community wishing to use this book to pray the psalms and canticles found in the *Liturgy of the Hours* for such occasions might simply locate the appropriate texts here by means of the index of psalms and canticles.

THE COMMUNITY AT PRAYER

In the days when the bonds of a common faith and a simpler geography brought neighbors together regularly, Christian communities quite naturally gathered to pray the daily hours, especially morning and evening. They were aware that the body of Christ must pray the prayer of Christ together in order to enter most deeply into the shared reality of our new humanity. Today we are invited to pray together, morning and evening, in whatever assemblies, small or large, we can create: in the household, among friends, with neighbors or co-workers. The psalms and canticles are our common cry of memory and hope, of praise and pain, of confidence and fear. We are brought together by the human realities they articulate; we can find one another's truth, as well as our own, in their lines. We are urged to pray for one another with their words.

When circumstance makes common prayer impossible, we can nevertheless transcend the barriers of physical separation and enter the deeper reality of the communion we share in Jesus Christ by uniting our prayer with that of the whole church through these texts. They demand of us that we rejoice with those who rejoice and weep with those who weep, whatever our personal mood of the moment. Through the psalms and canticles of Morning and Evening Prayer, our many voices are gathered together in the one prayer of Jesus Christ, whether we are in the same room or half a world apart. In praying thus together, we take our place with Christ, who intercedes always on our behalf before the throne of God's mercy. Thus is our prayer integral to our mission as church: to open the way for all humanity to make the common journey into the reign of God.

This book is essentially a psalter, a collection of psalms and canticles for use at the various times set aside for prayer in the Christian tradition. It does not dictate a particular style of prayer. The psalms may be prayed aloud or silently; they may be said or sung; they may be prayed by one person alone or by a group reading them together, or alternating verses, or listening to a single reader.

The book does make possible prayer that incorporates many dimensions of our human being. The pages are laid out in a medley of word and artwork and silent white space to invite us to pray with voice and eye, aloud and in the quiet of the heart. The psalms and canticles are pointed for singing to encourage us to allow the words, carried by simple repetitive melodies, to sink more deeply into our being than can the spoken word alone. Some of the psalms themselves prompt us to sing (for example, Psalm 95:1), or to incorporate the traditional postures of standing (Psalm 134:1) or kneeling (Psalm 95:6) or praying with uplifted hands (Psalm 141:2) into our individual or common prayer.

The book may be used by those who simply wish to pray the psalms. Some common hymn texts are appended for those who wish to supplement psalm and canticle with hymns. To use the book as part of a more extended act of prayer, such as the Liturgy of the Hours, one will need other resources for hymns, scripture readings and whatever additional prayers one might wish to add.

For those who wish to follow it, the ordinary structure of Morning Prayer as given in the *Liturgy of the Hours* is 1) a call to worship (in the form of an invitatory psalm, found here on page 262, with antiphons suitable to the different seasons of the church year); 2) a morning psalm, canticle, and psalm of praise, each with its antiphon; 3) a biblical reading; 4) the Canticle of Zechariah (page 265) with its antiphon; 5) intercessions with a particular focus on the dedication of the day to God; 6) the Lord's Prayer; 7) a closing prayer and blessing.

The structure of Evening Prayer is similar: 1) a hymn; 2) two psalms and a New Testament canticle, all with their antiphons; 3) a reading, usually taken from the New Testament; 4) the Canticle of Mary (page 267) with its antiphon; 5) intercessions; 6) the Lord's Prayer; 7) a closing prayer and blessing.

Midday Prayer is simpler, consisting of a hymn, psalm or psalms (see pages 234–47; antiphons are not given), short biblical reading and concluding prayer.

Night Prayer includes a short penitential rite, hymn, psalms (see pages 250–58; antiphons are not given), short reading, Canticle of Simeon (page 259) with antiphon (page 263), and closing prayer. After the final blessing, it is customary to sing a hymn to Mary, Mother of God.

Recommended readings, intercessions and concluding prayers for each hour, as well as more seasonal antiphons, may be found in any edition of the church's *Liturgy of the Hours* (in a communal setting, only the leader would need a copy of that book). The reader can use a Bible. And the remainder of the assembly needs only this book of psalms and canticles.

Jennifer Glen, CCVI

An Introduction to
THE TRANSLATION

T his translation of the Book of Psalms is a liturgical psalter, one intended for communal singing or recitation in public prayer. Prepared by the International Commission on English in the Liturgy, it can be distinguished in its style from other English language translations. Other English versions (the Grail version, the King James, the Jerusalem Bible or the Frost psalters, for example) have their own integrity, and there was no reason to prepare a translation that would imitate any one of them. The goal of this translation into modern English language poetry is to expose in our vernacular the power of the ancient psalter as a primer for contemporary prayer.

At an early stage of the work, a published poet among the collaborators wondered whether the honed and polished idiom of much biblical translation could ever be effectively cracked open. Could a translation ever recover for English speakers the original semitic metaphors rising from and giving voice to the experience of God's presence and God's absence? The poet's skepticism was a challenge: How do we get beyond well-loved but conventional turns of phrase to unleash the energy of the ancient Hebrew poems? How do we reveal in our contemporary English-speaking cultures the psalmist's keen awareness of divine presence and judgment in ordinary human experience? The comfort of familiar religious idiom and cadence is well known, but familiarity also has the effect of concealing as much as it reveals about the mystery of the divine-human encounter. Could a new translation of the psalms as religious poetry surprise us again into recognition?

CATHOLIC USE OF THE PSALTER

Each psalm is a poem. Whole psalms, complete poems, are used in the Liturgy of the Hours. But the majority of

Catholic worshipers know these ancient religious poems in parts rather than wholes, primarily through what is presented Sunday by Sunday as the responsorial psalm. Responsorial psalms in most instances excerpt selected phrases or verses from the biblical poems; the verses are then assigned to the liturgical day or the season because of their power to focus spiritual meaning. There is both gain and loss in this selected use of the psalms in our liturgical books. The gain is that the particular lines give the church heightened language to voice joy, confidence, grief or hope with an intensity appropriate to the liturgical occasion—funeral, ordinary time or paschal rejoicing. With such words regularly placed on our lips at prayer, corresponding sentiments form gradually in our hearts. In this way the psalm phrases become primer and tutor, expanding and guiding our religious sensibilities.

But concern for the integrity of the poetry confirmed the judgment that the whole psalm, not the shorter sections found in some of the liturgical books, was the unit for translation in this liturgical psalter. Whole psalms yield a certain surplus of religious meaning not available in separated lines and verses, because the poems frequently mix a range of religious feelings. Their complexity alerts us to the infinite mystery of the presence we seek, within which we dwell, with which we wrestle. The whole psalm, with whatever shifts of sensibility, mood and purpose, and whatever changes of speaker and addressee it registers, is the font of the discrete sentiments presented in excerpted antiphons and verses in liturgical books. Recovery of the spiritual power of any part of this ancient religious poetry is intimately tied to unlocking the energy of the whole.

HOW TO TRANSLATE A POEM

However distinctive this translation is as poetry, it is biblical translation and not paraphrase. Skilled translators, working from the Masoretic Hebrew text at all stages of the project, consulted the Septuagint and other major ancient versions. They drew on current research into ancient northwest Semitic philology, which has opened up new understandings of biblical Hebrew. But translation is an art, not an exact science. Translation can be informed by more than one set of principles for negotiating the moves from an ancient language to a modern one.

"Dynamic equivalence" and "formal equivalence" are two approaches to translation; they have the same goals: to give an accurate rendering of the original Hebrew text and to make complete sense in English, the "receptor language." But translators are always faced with the need to make judgments, because there is no perfect match between any two languages, and certainly no possibility of a perfect match between ancient Hebrew and contemporary English.

Formal equivalence seeks to honor the distinctive characteristics of the original language (e.g., grammatical constructions, word order, tense, number and gender markers, and so on). Faced with the differences in languages, the translator aiming for formal equivalence is prepared to accept whatever awkwardness results from putting the receptor language, English, to work in ways not suited to it. Dynamic equivalence, the approach used in this translation, shifts the weight in the other direction, preferring to honor the idiom of the receptor language, in this case English.

When the texts being translated are poetry, the need for judgment—whether to seek formal or dynamic equivalence—is heightened. Modern English poetry has many features in common with ancient Hebrew poetry, but the two poetic styles are not identical. A formal equivalence translation will seek to reproduce the Hebrew poetic form as closely as possible (for example, the celebrated parallelism of Hebrew poetry). This approach to translation will yield an Englished Hebrew poem, but not necessarily contemporary English poetry. A dynamic equivalence translation, by contrast, will move forward only those elements of the ancient poetic form that are congruent with contemporary English poetry; semitic parallelism will not make the linguistic crossing. Instead, the translator will employ equivalent English poetic strategies. The yield will be contemporary English poetry.

Some characteristics of this translation of the psalter for liturgical use can be noted briefly. First, while English is a complex language with a richly mixed ancestry, translators discovered that monosyllabic Anglo-Saxon English was more effective than polysyllabic English that had a Norman or Latinate lineage. Anglo-Saxon vocabulary best captured the direct and concise quality of the original Hebrew. It also served the unadorned directness of modern English poetry. So this version of Psalm 78 says in part:

> *The people stuffed their mouths,*
> *God satisfied their greed.*
> *But while they gorged themselves,*
> *cramming down their food,*
> *God's anger flared against them,*
> *destroying their sturdiest,*
> *striking down Israel's youth.*

The language used in the familiar Grail version is more muted:

> *So they ate and had their fill;*
> *for he gave them all they craved.*
> *But before they had sated their craving,*
> *while the food was still in their mouth,*
> *God's anger rose against them.*
> *He slew the strongest among them,*
> *struck down the flower of Israel.*

Compare "gorged themselves" and "sated their craving"; either is intelligible English idiom and each is a possible translation of the Hebrew. But the two phrases come from different ancestral lines of contemporary English, and their meanings are hardly identical.

The same passage from Psalm 78 points up a second characteristic of the English style of this translation. The poetic energy and immediacy found in the Hebrew verbs has been captured in the English verbs. Compare the cumulative effect of the words *stuffed, satisfied, gorged, cramming, flared, destroying* and *striking down* with the combination of verbs *ate, had, gave, craved, had sated, was, rose, slew, struck down*. They sound in different registers.

A third characteristic of this translation comes from the ambiguity and flexibility of Hebrew tenses relative to the English language tense system. Many Hebrew verbs commonly translated in the past tense have legitimately been rendered in the present tense. This gives greater immediacy to the psalms as prayer. Psalm 33:9 reads, "God speaks: the world is" as an alternative to the more familiar "By the Lord's word, the heavens were made." Theological truth is also served in this particular treatment of tense.

PSALMS FOR SINGING AND SAYING

This liturgical psalter is intended for communal singing or oral recitation, not for silent reading or for study. In oral literature the sounds of words and their sequences matter, both poetically and musically, and they contribute to the meaning. This translation presumes musical performance as the norm, although choral recitation will undoubtedly be widespread in groups that pray the psalms daily in the Liturgy of the Hours. But musicians are encouraged to use their musical genius to make these texts sing as prayers, to make them memorable for praying communities. If the translation is to accomplish its purpose, the texts will need composers from the wide variety of cultural and social backgrounds that constitute the English-speaking church.

The distinctive style of this psalter—fewer, terser words expressing heightened meaning, and ideas that move forward without providing for a pause at the end of every line—will challenge the familiar expectations of composers and of communities faithful to daily choral recitation in other translations. These psalms have a firm rhythmic structure (the musicians who worked throughout the project saw to that), but the number of unaccented syllables in each line of poetry has been deliberately reduced. As contemporary English poetry, this language is spare. One consequence is that many available psalm tones—those composed for use with the Grail texts, for example, that assume a proportionately higher ration of unaccented to accented syllables—will be a poor fit for the new texts. Composers will need to write simpler tones. Racing choirs used to gliding on frequent unaccented syllables will be required to change their gait.

But composers will want to write more than new chant tones. The various poetic genres found in the psalter—hymns of praise, laments, litanies, historical narratives, songs of thanksgiving, didactic acrostics, dramatic liturgies, and so on—invite different musical treatments and even expanded liturgical use. For example, where a liturgical book designates the use of selected psalm verses for a responsorial psalm (e.g., verses from Psalm 22 on Good Friday) the creative composer may engage an assembly, its choir and its cantors in singing the whole.

GENDER IN THE PSALTER

The psalm translators also have attended to the ongoing developments in English gender usage and to contemporary theological discussions about gender in traditional religious language. Such attention involved, first of all, a commitment to overcome conventional lapses into what

has been called "translator's bias," the unexamined prefer-
ence for male pronouns and male-centered images and
metaphors even when these were not warranted by the
original text. Principles of either formal or dynamic equivalence would have required this much.

Translation according to principles of dynamic equivalence
raised other questions about gendered language in the
psalter. Where do women stand in the story of salvation?
Were the women of Israel parties to covenant blessing?
Were they fully present to events recounted in the biblical
story of salvation, even while the language used later to
recount Israel's meeting with the living God concealed
them? Was it God or the story-telling men of the Hebrew
peoples who marginalized women at Sinai? Who is the
mysterious God whose name, made known to Moses, could
not be pronounced, and to whom Israel's leaders gave other
names and titles now canonized with the biblical text?

Because there are not yet any sustained models for gender-
sensitive Bible translation, principles for dealing with gender issues in the translation evolved as translators faced
particular textual challenges. Judgments—theological, historical, socio-cultural, linguistic and literary—were made
again and again and reconsidered again and again as the
identity of the human subjects of the psalter and the
identity of God both came under scrutiny.

The treatment of some texts was self-evident. Psalm 45
assumes the existence of certain historic social institutions:

Your sons will inherit
the throne your fathers held.

The translators let that stand. They made no effort to
rewrite either history or the psalm. Moreover, where the
feminine personification of Zion (and the accompanying
implicit feminization of the chosen people relative to a

divine masculine) is integral to the imagery of a poem, as in Psalm 87, translators worked with the poem's own operative convention of making the city feminine, so "Zion mothered each and every one." Without the metaphor there is no poem.

Such historic institutions and conventional metaphors do not dominate all genres of the psalms. A more typical feature of many psalms is their presumptive male world. The poems' identification of worshipers or plaintiffs as the men of Israel is predicated on the bond of male covenant membership sealed by circumcision. This in turn was the basis for participation in the temple cult, for which the biblical book of 150 psalms was collected and edited over many generations.

That temple-based perspective conceals the memory, recorded many places elsewhere in the Bible, that women of Israel were also song writers and leaders of song. Miriam comes to mind (Exodus 15:20–21), as do Hannah (1 Samuel 2:1–10) and Judith (16:1–17). Commentators on the Book of Exodus tell us the song fragment attributed to Miriam is perhaps the most ancient of all the songs of Israel. Women sang praise and thanks, voiced trust, lamented the people's sufferings and their own. They honored wisdom and celebrated salvation in song, and they were credited with doing so.

On the basis of this internal evidence from the biblical tradition, this translation makes the judgment that the psalms are Hebrew prayers composed and sung by women and men alike, even though that is not immediately evident in the psalter as it has come to us. If the broader truth about Israel's songs had been forgotten in the course of the collecting and editing and handing on of Israel's psalms as "the Psalms of David" in the service of the Jerusalem temple cult, and if the Hebrew employs language conventions like the exclusive use of masculine pronouns, the translators became responsible for appropriate critical handling of texts in this dynamic equivalence translation for contemporary prayer.

Sometimes inclusive translations of the ancient texts came easily. Depending on the internal dynamics of particular texts, each with its own organizing metaphors and shifts of voice and number, the translators may have rendered a nonspecific "he" as an "I" or "we," or a "you" or "they," or even a "whoever."

Yet the fact is there to be wrestled with as vigorously as Jacob ever wrestled with God: Insofar as the biblical texts are historical expressions of the human reception of divine revelation, it is not possible to excise the human social reality of patriarchy from the world of the psalms and still claim to be translating these ancient texts. Something else is possible: to deal with the large set of heretofore unexamined conventions in biblical translation that have made praying the psalms different for people newly convinced that men and women can and must worship together in spirit and in truth.

SPEAKING OF GOD IN PRAYER

Naming God in the psalms introduced additional challenges for the translators. The Hebrew texts offer *Elohim* (God) and *Adoni* (Lord). For two reasons, translators ruled out simply restoring the concealed divine name *YHWH* (I Am Who Am) that lies behind the Hebrew *Adoni*. First, it would have been incongruous to introduce into the translation an archaism that would need extensive explanation for those using this psalter for communal prayer. Second, such a solution failed to regard the religious sensibilities of Jews who, out of reverence, do not pronounce the ancient name in their prayer. But how, then, was *Adoni* to be translated?

This psalter used "God" and "Lord" interchangeably in the English translations, except where context clearly requires one or the other. This flexibility is warranted by the Hebrew text itself, which often uses the two words as synonymous in parallel lines. The flexibility was required by the concise literary style; frequent uses of the phrase "the Lord" had metrical consequences.

Because the connotative freight of the words "lord" and "Lord" has been the subject of extended discussion in many communities of biblical faith, the use of both "God" and "Lord" was reconsidered multiple times. At one stage the translators explored the possibility of using only "God." The solution was justifiable on internal textual grounds. It is a fact well known to scholars that a subcollection within the Book of Psalms (42–83) has been edited for religious reasons in some unremembered past, so that "Lord" had been suppressed and "Elohim" or "God" stands as the now-forgotten editor's name of choice. Should this ancient editorial work of suppressing *Adoni* for religious reasons have been brought to completion? After repeated reconsideration, that path was not taken.

Is "Lord" as a name for divine mystery wholly unacceptable to that part of the praying church that is consciously struggling to become a discipleship of equals? Does "Lord" as a divine name inevitably divinize maleness and patriarchal relationships? In the United States "lord" has no secular currency whatsoever in the local culture. For Catholics, the word operates as part of the religious vocabulary of a community that officially recognizes only male leadership and nonparticipatory governance as "the will of the Lord."

Other English speakers in the North Atlantic who were involved in the translation work and will be involved in the praying of these psalms reported that "lord" carries less freight with them because the word gets more varied use. For example, the honorific "Lord Mayor" is used for women holding that public office in Scotland, England and Ireland. In the socio-cultural world of these praying communities, "lord" denotes and connotes public office held by either males or females that involves public participation in its exercise.

The translators knew also that the National Council of Churches of North America had faced the question of the religious and secular connotations and denotations of "Lord" earlier in its preparation of its inclusive language lectionary. Voices from the historical African American churches dissented from the early proposal in that project to eliminate "Lord" in public proclamation. They dissented on the basis of their own social history. Oppression and oppressors they knew well enough, but the oppressor they endured had not been the one they called "Lord." While lording it over others was white people's sin, "Lord Jesus" and "King Jesus" had kept black people's hopes alive. So in these churches, the psalms sing of a Lordship that transcended the oppression of their white, church-going slave masters and mistresses. In the vocabulary of African American Christians, "Lord" has strong christological overtones and speaks concretely of deliverance from oppressors.

So what's in a L(l)ord? The "Lord" of the psalms and the psalmists was also reflected on, and the poems themselves give complex witness. The disclosure is regularly in the Hebrew verbs, which are vividly anthropomorphic. They reveal the mystery of a personal "God who acts," one caught up by choice in the history of the human race. But this mystery is divine: personal existence that embraces and transcends gendered human existence, and yet is open to being imaged in all human actions. In Psalm 68, for example, a playful God "rides the clouds" and "blew kings about like snow on Mount Zalmon." But then in the same hymn turned destructive and "smashed the heads of the enemies, the skulls of the guilty." Divine play and destruction are anthropomorphic, but neither play nor destruction are gender based. The divine mystery is personal; yet here is another mystery: personhood that is not gendered.

Other psalm texts also disclose divine gender-fullness in conventional terms. The poet of Psalm 17 can imagine the "Lord" as maternal, and asks:

Guard me under your wings,
hide me from those who attack,
from predators who surround me.

Later, the same psalmist speaks of the mystery of the Lord God reflected in the bonding moment that modern developmental psychologists see as the basis for all human trust, mother and child locked in the intimate gaze that foreshadows all future human intimacy. The poet, anticipating such intimacy with God, writes:

I will then be justified,
will wake to see your face,
and be filled with your presence.

In Psalm 68 the writer credits the "Lord" with social services we usually relegate to women, with work not considered "manly" by our contemporary social and political standards.

Further, this odd warrior "Lord" who has power to set straight persistent social disorder does not depend exclusively on male collaborators:

God speaks a word;
a company of women
spreads the good news.

Psalm 68, like Psalm 17, sings of a Lord unafraid of female form and female companions in undertaking saving deeds.

But in Psalm 89, a cultic celebration of the Davidic covenant, King David's vision of God bypasses these "unconventional" womanly experiences of divine-human intimacy in favor of a more manly one. In this song, the psalmist depicts God narrating a first-person experience of forming a covenant relationship with David:

> *He calls out to me: "My father,*
> *my God, my rock of safety!"*
> *I respond: "My firstborn,*
> *noblest of kings."*

David's man-to-man experience of God is certainly part of the memory of divine-human intimacy recorded in the psalms, but it is not the whole.

The anthropomorphic God of the psalms uncovered in this new English translation is worthy of sustained attention on the part of both biblical theologians and praying communities interested in relief from gender reductionism. If the language for God in any single psalm or in all of them together fails to meet every human expectation, this translation may be onto something. No single image or metaphor taken in isolation reveals the mystery of the divine celebrated in the psalms; the only true name of God is one we are forbidden to say. Language collapses before the mystery of divine fullness. YHWH's identity is like nothing in the heavens above or on the earth below. The "one who is" will be "who will be," causing to be whatever comes to be!

Still, it must be acknowledged that the final text of this psalter is a skin only three-quarters full of new wine. Once the project had been completed, ICEL forwarded the psalter to the Catholic Bishops' Committee on Doctrine for the imprimatur, which that body gives for biblical translations being published in the United States. The Committee on Doctrine reported back that it had decided earlier "in principle" that it would not give the imprimatur to any biblical translation, however successful, that had avoided calling God "he." The principle at issue, presumably theological but perhaps more mundane, was not elaborated. Anticlimactically, the translators returned to undo some of their original work. The version published here is the result: All involved wanted to get this psalter in circulation even in a compromised form. But this liturgical psalter is published as a study text, inviting your comments. Those who pray these psalms may want to enter deeply into prayerful reflection on the gender issues that challenge the church today. A second edition may finally present the text that was intended for publication now.

AN OLD CHRISTIAN TRADITION

Christians adopted the psalter as a primer for prayer in the second and third centuries. In company with the gospels, the psalms have formed the religious sensibilities of countless Christian generations since then. This translation aims to keep that tradition alive into the twenty-first century. Strong images received and savored in prayer will lead to insight; and religious insight brings with it an invitation to repentance and conversion, to praise and gratitude, to gracious service of the poor in search of justice, and to humble acceptance of unavoidable and unfathomable suffering. With the help of the musicians who will set these texts for use in common prayer, this psalter may sing the church into new recognition of the mystery of God, which is also the mystery of Christ, at work in ordinary life.

Mary Collins, OSB

An Introduction to
THE PSALM TONES

T o make possible the singing of this translation of the psalms and canticles, this book provides a psalm tone for the Canticles of Mary and Zechariah, a psalm tone for the Canticle of Simeon, a psalm tone for Psalm 95, and nine psalm tones for the singing of the other canticles and psalms.

With the exception of the tone for the Canticle of Simeon, which has only two sections, each of the psalm tones has four sections, designated A, B, C and D. Each section consists of a reciting note (◘), followed by two preparatory notes (• ●) and a concluding note (○).

The concluding note must coincide with the last stressed syllable of the line of psalm text. If this syllable is followed by other syllables, they are sung on the same note.

The two syllables before the last stressed syllable will ordinarily be sung on the two preparatory notes. Thus, the second to last syllable before the final stressed syllable is pointed with a straight underline mark as in the following examples from Psalm 51:18–19.

> When I offer a holocaust,
> the gift does not please you.
> So I offer my shattered spirit;
> a changed heart you welcome.

In some instances where the syllable before the final stressed syllable in the line also receives a stress, two straight underline marks will be found under that syllable to indicate that the two preparatory notes are to be sung on that one syllable. Here are several examples:

> in Jerusalem give praise (Tobit 13:8)
> scattered at the grave's edge (Psalm 141:7)
> God breathes: the stars shine (Psalm 33:6)

Each stanza is pointed according to the sense of the text. In some instances, a section or measure of the tone is sung for each line of a four-line stanza. But at times the sense of a stanza requires that only two sections of the tone be used, as in verse 8 from Psalm 19:

> God's perfect law
> revives the soul.
> God's stable rule
> guides the simple.

In this case, section A of the tone is sung for the first two lines and section D of the tone for the last two lines. When the sense or structure of the text calls for only three underline marks within a stanza, sections A, B and D of the tone are used as in stanza 1, verses 1 to 3, of Psalm 136:

> Our God is good, give thanks!
> God's love is for ever!
> Our God of gods, give thanks!
> God's love is for ever!
> Our Lord of lords, give thanks!
> God's love is for ever!

To summarize: In stanzas with two underline marks, sections A and D of the tone are used; in stanzas with three underline marks, sections A, B and D are used; and in stanzas with four underline marks, all four sections of the tone are used. If a stanza consists of only one line, for the purpose of sung recitations that line is sung twice, the first time to section A of the tone, the second to section D. This applies in the case of verse 18 of Exodus 15, which stands on its own as a separate stanza:

> The Lord rules for ever and ever!

For the convenience of those using the tones, each tone is presented (see pages xlix to lvii) in three formats: with all four sections (A, B, C and D), with three sections (A, B and D), and with two sections (A and D). Roman numerals "I" and "II" indicate two alternative accompaniments for each tone. If desired, the two can be used to accompany alternate stanzas of a psalm.

In the sung recitation of the psalms and canticles to the tones contained in this book, the texts should be sung as they would be spoken in good, clear speech. Singers should follow the sense, the punctuation and the natural rhythm of the text. They should avoid, for example, making the syllables all equal in length or falsely accenting the concluding note at the end of the line.

A different tone has been composed for each genre of text. Thus, for example, tone 1 has been composed for those psalms that are like hymns, tone 3 for individual laments, tone 5 for communal laments and tone 9 for prophetic exhortations. An index assigning a particular tone to each psalm or canticle is provided on the following pages. Over time, a community will become familiar with all nine tones. Because the tones all follow the same rules for pointing and singing, a community can begin by selecting and learning only several of the nine tones. Gradually a community may learn additional tones until all nine tones are known and are used with the proper psalms.

Peter Finn

PSALM TONE INDEX

In the following list, the psalms found in this book are given in their sequence from the Book of Psalms and the canticles in their sequence from the Bible.

Each psalm and canticle is assigned a tone (see the explanation of the tones on the previous pages and the tones themselves on the pages that follow). Because each tone was composed to reflect a particular genre of psalm, the tones here assigned try to place each psalm within its genre.

PSALM TONE INDEX

PSALM TONE INDEX

THE PSALM TONES

Tone 1: The Hymns

Howard Hughes, SM © 1992 ICEL

Tone 2: Hymns of the Lord's Kingship and Songs of Zion

Howard Hughes, SM © 1992 ICEL

Tone 3: Laments of an Individual

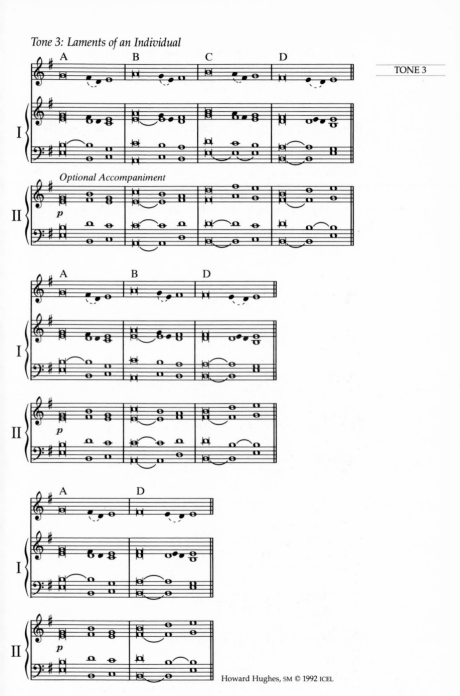

Howard Hughes, SM © 1992 ICEL

Tone 4: Confidence or Thanksgiving of an Individual

Howard Hughes, SM © 1992 ICEL

Tone 5: Laments of the Community

Optional Accompaniment

Howard Hughes, SM © 1992 ICEL

Tone 6: Confidence or Thanksgiving of the Community

Optional Accompaniment

Howard Hughes, SM © 1992 ICEL

Tone 7: Royal Psalms

Howard Hughes, SM © 1992 ICEL

Tone 8: Wisdom and Historical Psalms

Optional Accompaniment

Howard Hughes, SM © 1992 ICEL

Tone 9: Prophetic Exhortations and Liturgies

Howard Hughes, SM © 1992 ICEL

Invitatory

PSALM TONE

Howard Hughes, SM © 1992 ICEL

PSALM 95

Come, sing with joy to God,
shout to our savior, our rock.
Enter God's presence with praise,
enter with shouting and song.

A great God is the Lord,
over the gods like a king.
God cradles the depths of the earth,
holds fast the mountain peaks.
God shaped the ocean and owns it,
formed the earth by hand.

Come, bow down and worship,
kneel to the Lord our maker.
This is our God, our shepherd,
we are the flock led with care.

Listen today to God's voice:
"Harden no heart as at Meribah,
on that day in the desert at Massah.
There your people tried me,
though they had seen my work.

"Forty years with that lot!
I said: They are perverse,
they do not accept my ways.
So I swore in my anger:
They shall not enter my rest." □

Canticle of Simeon

Howard Hughes, SM © 1992 ICEL

Lord, let your servant
now die in peace,
for you kept your promise.

With my own eyes
I see the salvation
you prepared for all peoples:

a light of revelation for the Gentiles
and glory to your people Israel. □

Antiphons for Canticles of Mary and Zechariah

CANTICLE OF MARY

I ac-claim the great-ness of the Lord, I de-light in God my sav - ior.

Howard Hughes, SM © 1992 ICEL

CANTICLE OF ZECHARIAH

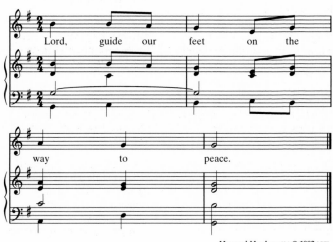

Lord, guide our feet on the way to peace.

Howard Hughes, SM © 1992 ICEL

Howard Hughes, SM © 1992 ICEL

PSALM TONE

Optional Accompaniment

I

II

CANTICLE
OF MARY

I acclaim the greatness of the Lord,
I delight in God my savior,
who regarded my humble state.
Truly from this day on
all ages will call me blest.

For God, wonderful in power,
has used that strength for me.
Holy the name of the Lord!
whose mercy embraces the faithful,
one generation to the next.

The mighty arm of God
scatters the proud in their conceit,
pulls tyrants from their thrones,
and raises up the humble.
The Lord fills the starving
and lets the rich go hungry.

God rescues lowly Israel,
recalling the promise of mercy,
the promise made to our ancestors,
to Abraham's heirs for ever. □

CANTICLE OF
ZECHARIAH

Praise the Lord, the God of Israel,
who shepherds the people
    and sets them free.

God raises from David's house
a child with power to save.
Through the holy prophets
God promised in ages past
to save us from enemy hands,
from the grip of all who hate us.

The Lord favored our ancestors
recalling the sacred covenant,
the pledge to our ancestor Abraham,

to free us from our enemies,
so we might worship without fear
and be holy and just all our days.

And you, child, will be called
Prophet of the Most High,
for you will come to prepare
a pathway for the Lord
by teaching the people salvation
through forgiveness of their sin.

Out of God's deepest mercy
a dawn will come from on high,
light for those shadowed by death,
a guide for our feet on the
    way to peace. □

PSALM TONES

lxi

COMMON HYMNS

Now that the daylight fills the sky,
We lift our hearts to God on high,
That God in all we do or say,
Would keep us free from harm today.

O Lord, restrain our tongues from strife,
From wrath and anger shield our life;
And guard with watchful care our eyes
That we will choose from all that's wise.

O may our inmost hearts be pure,
From thoughts of folly kept secure,
And all our pow'rs devoted be
To deeds of love that keep us free.

So we, when this day's work is o'er,
And shades of night return once more,
Our path of trial safely trod,
Shall give the glory to our God.

All praise to God the Father be,
And praise the Son eternally,
Whom with the Spirit we adore,
One God alone, for evermore.

Jam lucis orto sidere, 8th century.
Translated by John Mason Neale
and others. From *Resource Collection
of Hymns and Service Music for the
Liturgy,* © 1981, International Committee
on English in the Liturgy, Inc. All
rights reserved.
LM

This day God gives me
Strength of high heaven,
Sun and moon shining,
Flame in my hearth,
Flashing of lightning,
Wind in its swiftness,
Deeps of the ocean,
Firmness of earth.

This day God sends me
Strength as my guardian,
Might to uphold me,
Wisdom as guide.
Your eyes are watchful,
Your ears are list'ning,
Your lips are speaking,
Friend at my side.

God's way is my way,
God's shield is round me,
God's host defends me,
Saving from ill.
Angels of heaven,
Drive from me always
All that would harm me,
Stand by me still.

Rising, I thank you,
Mighty and strong One,
King of creation,
Giver of rest,
Firmly confessing
Threeness of Persons,
Oneness of Godhead,
Trinity blest.

"This day God gives me" Text: *St. Patrick's
Breastplate,* 8th cent. Tr. by James Quinn, SJ, 1968, ©.
Used by permission of Selah Publishing Co., Inc.,
Kingston, N.Y. All rights reserved.
Tune: BUNESSAN, 5, 5, 5, 4, D.

O radiant Light, O sun divine
Of God the Father's deathless face,
O Image of the light sublime
That fills the heav'nly dwelling place.

O Son of God, the source of life,
Praise is your due by night and day:
Our happy lips must raise the strain
Of your esteemed and splendid name.

Lord Jesus Christ, as daylight fades,
As shine the lights of eventide,
We praise the Father with the Son,
The Spirit blest and with them one.

Phos hilaron, Greek, 3rd century.
Translation © William G. Storey.
LM

O splendor of eternal light,
Who in full glory dwell on high!
The world began as light from Light,
All goodness in the Father's sight.

Upon the twilight chaos played
Your Wisdom forming night and day.
As night descends to you we sing
To hover near on brooding wing.

Forgive the sins we cannot bear,
Lest, overwhelmed by earthly care,
The mind forget eternal life,
And dwell in exile from its light.

Let heaven's Spirit pulse within
To purge the memory of sin;
Thus, casting off forgetful night,
We rise enrobed with firstborn light.

Almighty Father, hear our cry
Through Jesus Christ our Lord most high,
Whom in the Spirit we adore,
Who reigns with you for evermore.

Lucis Creator optime, 7th century.
Translated by Paul Quenon, OCSO,
© Abbey of Gethsemani.
LM

Day is done, but love unfailing
Dwells ever here;
Shadows fall, but hope, prevailing,
Calms ev'ry fear.
Loving Father, none forsaking,
Take our hearts, of love's own making,
Watch our sleeping, guard our waking,
Be always near!

Dark descends, but light unending
Shines through our night;
You are with us, ever lending
New strength to sight;
One in love, your truth confessing,
One in hope of heaven's blessing,
May we see, in love's possessing,
Love's endless light!

Eyes will close, but you, unsleeping,
Watch by our side;
Death may come: in love's safe keeping
Still we abide.
God of love, all evil quelling,
Sin forgiving, fear dispelling,
Stay with us, our hearts indwelling,
This eventide!

"Day is done" Text: James Quinn, SJ, 1969, ©.
Used by permission of Selah Publishing Co.,
Inc., Kingston, N.Y. All rights reserved.
Tune: AR HYD Y NOS, 84 84 88 84.

God, who made the earth and heaven,
Darkness and light:
You the day for work have given,
For rest the night.
May your angel guards defend us,
Slumber sweet your mercy send us,
Holy dreams and hopes attend us,
All through the night.

And when morn again shall call us
To run life's way,
May we still whate'er befall us,
Your will obey.
From the pow'r of evil hide us,
In the narrow pathway guide us,
Never be your smile denied us
All through the day.

Guard us waking, guard us sleeping,
And, when we die,
May we in your mighty keeping
All peaceful lie.
When the last dread call shall wake us,
Then, O Lord, do not forsake us,
But to reign in glory take us
With you on high.

Stanza 1, R. Heber; stanza 2, W. Mercer;
stanza 3, R. Whately, alt.
Tune: AR HYD Y NOS, 84 84 88 84.

SUNDAY
Week I

SUNDAY EVENING PRAYER I

Let my prayer rise like incense,
my upraised hands, like an evening sacrifice.

Hurry, Lord! I call and call!
Listen! I plead with you.
Let my prayer rise like incense,
my upraised hands, like an evening sacrifice.

Lord, guard my lips,
watch my every word.
Let me never speak evil
or consider hateful deeds,
let me never join the wicked
to eat their lavish meals.

If the just correct me,
I take their rebuke as kindness,
but the unction of the wicked
will never touch my head.
I pray and pray
against their hateful ways.

Let them be thrown
against a rock of judgment,
then they will know
I spoke the truth.
Then they will say,
"Our bones lie broken upon the ground,
scattered at the grave's edge."

Lord my God, I turn to you,
in you I find safety.
Do not strip me of life.
Do not spring on me
the traps of the wicked.
Let evildoers get tangled
in their own nets,
but let me escape. □

You are my refuge, God,
all I have in the land of the living.

I pray, I plead,
I cry for mercy, Lord;
I pour out all my troubles,
the story of my distress.
My spirit fails me.

You know the road I walk
and the traps hidden from me.
See what they are doing!
No one befriends me
or cares for me.

There is no escape,
so I turn to you, Lord.
I know you are my refuge,
all I have in the land of the living.

I am pleading, hear me!
I have no strength.
God, rescue me!
They hunt me down,
and overwhelm me.

Free me from this cage!
Then I will praise your name
and gather with the just
to thank you for your kindness. □

<table>
<tr><td>PHILIPPIANS
2:6 – 11</td><td>Jesus humbled himself
and God lifted him high.</td></tr>
</table>

Though in the form of God,
Jesus did not claim
equality with God
but emptied himself,
taking the form of a slave,
human like one of us.

Flesh and blood,
he humbled himself,
obeying to the death,
death on a cross.

For this very reason
God lifted him high
and gave him the name
above all names.

So at the name of Jesus
every knee will bend
in heaven, on earth,
and in the world below,
and every tongue exclaim
to the glory of God the Father,
"Jesus Christ is Lord." □

I acclaim the greatness of the Lord,
I delight in God my savior...

CANTICLE
OF MARY

SUNDAY MORNING PRAYER

As morning breaks I look to you, O God,
to be my strength this day, hallelujah.

God, my God, you I crave;
my soul thirsts for you,
my body aches for you
like a dry and weary land.
Let me gaze on you in your temple:
a vision of strength and glory.

Your love is better than life,
my speech is full of praise.
I give you a lifetime of worship,
my hands raised in your name.
I feast at a rich table,
my lips sing of your glory.

On my bed I lie awake,
your memory fills the night.
You have been my help,
I rejoice beneath your wings.
Yes, I cling to you,
your right hand holds me fast.

Let those who want me dead
end up deep in the grave!
They will die by the sword,
their bodies food for jackals.
But let the king find joy in God.
All who swear the truth be praised,
every lying mouth be shut. □

From the midst of the flames
the three young men cried out with one voice:
Blessed be God, hallelujah.

DANIEL 3:
56 – 88

Bless God beyond the stars.
Give praise and glory.
Bless God, heaven and earth.
Give praise and glory for ever.

Bless God, angels of God.
Give praise and glory.
Bless God, highest heavens.
Give praise and glory.

Bless God, waters above.
Give praise and glory.
Bless God, spirits of God.
Give praise and glory.

Bless God, sun and moon.
Give praise and glory.
Bless God, stars of heaven.
Give praise and glory for ever.

Bless God, rainstorm and dew.
Give praise and glory.
Bless God, gales and winds.
Give praise and glory.

Bless God, fire and heat.
Give praise and glory.
Bless God, frost and cold.
Give praise and glory.

Bless God, dew and snow.
Give praise and glory.
Bless God, ice and cold.
Give praise and glory.

Bless God, frost and sleet.
Give praise and glory.
Bless God, night and day.
Give praise and glory.

Bless God, light and darkness.
Give praise and glory.
Bless God, lightning and clouds.
Give praise and glory for ever.

Bless God, earth and sea.
Give praise and glory.
Bless God, mountains and hills.
Give praise and glory.

Bless God, trees and plants.
Give praise and glory.
Bless God, fountains and springs.
Give praise and glory.

Bless God, rivers and seas.
Give praise and glory.
Bless God, fishes and whales.
Give praise and glory.

Bless God, birds of the air.
Give praise and glory.
Bless God, beasts of the earth.
Give praise and glory for ever.

Bless God, children of earth.
Give praise and glory.
Bless God, Israel.
Give praise and glory.

Bless God, priests of God.
Give praise and glory.
Bless God, servants of God.
Give praise and glory.

Bless God, just and faithful souls.
Give praise and glory.
Bless God, holy and humble hearts.
Give praise and glory.
Bless God, Hananiah, Azariah, and Mishael.
Give praise and glory for ever.

Bless God beyond the stars.
Give praise and glory.
Bless God, heaven and earth.
Give praise and glory for ever. □

PSALM 149

Sing a new song, you faithful,
praise God in the assembly, hallelujah.

Sing a new song, you faithful,
praise God in the assembly.
Israel, rejoice in your maker,
Zion, in your king.
Dance in the Lord's name,
sounding harp and tambourine.

The Lord delights
in saving a helpless people.
Revel in God's glory,
join in clan by clan.
Shout praise from your throat,
sword flashing in hand

to discipline nations
and punish the wicked,
to shackle their kings
and chain their leaders,
and execute God's sentence.
You faithful, this is your glory!

Hallelujah! □

CANTICLE OF ZECHARIAH

Praise the Lord, the God of Israel,
who shepherds the people and sets them free...

SUNDAY EVENING PRAYER II

I will raise your scepter
over Zion and beyond, hallelujah.

The Lord decrees to the king:
"Take the throne at my right hand,
I will make your enemies a footrest.
I will raise your scepter
over Zion and beyond,
over all your enemies.

"Your people stand behind you
on the day you take command.
You are made holy, splendid,
newborn like the dawn,
fresh like the dew."

God's oath is firm:
"You are a priest for ever,
the rightful king by my decree."
The Lord stands at your side
to destroy kings
on the day of wrath.

God executes judgment,
crushes the heads of nations,
and brings carnage worldwide.
The victor drinks
from a wayside stream
and rises refreshed. □

Tremble! earth, before the Lord,
before the God of Jacob.

Israel marches out of Egypt,
Jacob leaves an alien people.
Judah becomes a holy place,
Israel, God's domain.

The sea pulls back for them,
the Jordan flees in retreat.
Mountains jump like rams,
hills like lambs in fear.

Why shrink back, O sea?
Jordan, why recoil?
Why shudder, mountains, like rams?
Why quiver, hills, like lambs?

Tremble! earth, before the Lord,
before the God of Jacob,
who turns rock to water,
flint to gushing streams. □

The Lord God almighty rules, alleluia!

Alleluia! (*or:* Amen. Alleluia!)
Salvation, glory and power to God!
Alleluia, Alleluia!
Right and sure, the judgments of God!
Alleluia, Alleluia!

Alleluia!
Praise our God, you faithful servants!
Alleluia, Alleluia!
In awe praise God, you small and great!
Alleluia, Alleluia!

Alleluia!
The Lord God almighty rules!
Alleluia, Alleluia!
Be glad, rejoice, give glory to God!
Alleluia, Alleluia!

Alleluia!
The wedding feast of the Lamb begins.
Alleluia, Alleluia!
The bride is radiant, clothed in glory.
Alleluia, Alleluia! (*or:* Amen. Alleluia!) □

Christ carried our sins in his body;
when he was wounded, we were healed.

1 PETER 2:
21 – 24

In Lent

Christ suffered for us
leaving us an example,
that we might walk
in his footsteps.

He did nothing wrong;
no false word
ever passed his lips.

When they cursed him
he returned no curse.
Tortured, he made no threats
but trusted in the perfect judge.

He carried our sins
in his body
to the cross,
that we might die to sin
and live for justice.
When he was wounded,
we were healed. □

I acclaim the greatness of the Lord,
I delight in God my savior...

MONDAY MORNING PRAYER

PSALM 5

I pray to you, Lord,
my prayer rises with the sun.

Hear my words, my groans,
my cries for help,
O God my king.
I pray to you, Lord,
my prayer rises with the sun.
At dawn I plead my case and wait.

You never welcome evil, God,
never let it stay.
You hate arrogance
and abhor scoundrels,
you detest violence
and destroy the traitor.

But by your great mercy
I enter your house
and bend low in awe
within your holy temple.

In the face of my enemies
clear the way,
bring me your justice.

Their charges are groundless,
they breathe destruction;
their tongues are smooth,
their throat an open grave.

God, pronounce them guilty,
catch them in their own plots,
expel them for their sins;
they have betrayed you.

But let those who trust you
be glad and celebrate for ever.
Protect those who love your name,
then they will delight in you.

For you bless the just, O God,
your grace surrounds them like a shield. □

1 CHRONICLES
29:10 – 13

God, we praise your splendid name.

Blest are you for ever, Lord,
God of our father Israel.
Power, splendor, greatness,
glory and honor are yours.

The whole universe is yours.
You are peerless in majesty,
from you flow wealth and glory.

You command all:
your hand is strength,
your hand makes strong.

And so we thank you, God,
we praise your splendid name. □

Give glory to God,
honor God's name.

Give the Lord glory, you spirits!
Give glory! Honor God's strength!
Honor the name of the Lord!
Bow when the Lord comes,
majestic and holy.

God's voice thunders
above the massive seas;
powerful, splendid,
God shatters the cedars,
shatters the cedars of Lebanon,
makes Lebanon jump like a calf,
Sirion like a wild ox.

God's voice strikes fire,
makes the desert shudder,
Qadesh shudder in labor,
deer writhe in labor.
God strips the trees.

All shout "Glory" in your temple, Lord.
For you rule the mighty waters,
you rule over all for ever.
Give strength to your people, Lord,
and bless your people with peace. □

Praise the Lord, the God of Israel,
who shepherds the people and sets them free...

CANTICLE OF
ZECHARIAH

MONDAY EVENING PRAYER

God looks tenderly on those who are poor.

I have taken shelter in God,
so how can you say to me:
"Go, fly like a bird to the hills,
for the wicked bend their bows,
lock their arrows on the string
to shoot the just from the shadows.
When the world falls apart,
what can the good hope to do?"

God dwells in his holy temple,
the heavens hold God's throne;
the Lord watches the earth,
eyes fixed on all nations,
weighing both righteous and wicked,
rejecting the violent.
God sends a rain of fire,
allots them a scorching wind.

The Lord loves justice,
the just will see God's face. □

Blest are the pure of heart,
for they shall see God.

Lord, who is welcome in your house?
Who can rest on your holy mountain?

Those who walk with integrity
and do only what is right,
speaking the truth with courage.

They never spread slander
or abuse their friends
or condemn their neighbors.

They disdain the godless,
but honor those who believe.
Before God, they give their word
and keep it at any cost.

They neither lend for gain
nor take bribes against the guiltless.
These are the just:
they stand for ever unshaken. □

God determined out of love
to adopt us through Jesus Christ.

EPHESIANS 1:
3 – 10

Bless God, the Father of our Lord Jesus Christ,
who blessed us from heaven through Christ
with every blessing of the Spirit.

Before laying the world's foundation,
God chose us in Christ
to live a pure and holy life.

God determined out of love
to adopt us through Jesus Christ
for the praise and glory of that grace
granted us in the Beloved.

By Christ's blood we were redeemed,
our sins forgiven
through extravagant love.

With perfect wisdom and insight
God freely displayed the mystery
of what was always intended:
a plan for the fullness of time
to unite the entire universe through Christ. □

<table>
<tr><td>CANTICLE
OF MARY</td><td>I acclaim the greatness of the Lord,
I delight in God my savior...</td></tr>
</table>

TUESDAY MORNING PRAYER

Whoever has integrity
shall climb the mountain of God.

God owns this planet
and all its riches.
The earth and every creature
belong to God.

God set the land on top of the seas
and anchored it in the deep.

Who is fit to climb God's mountain
and stand in his holy place?

Whoever has integrity:
not chasing shadows,
not living lies.

God will bless them,
their savior will bring justice.
These people long to see the Lord,
they seek the face of Jacob's God.

Stretch toward heaven, you gates,
open high and wide.
Let the glorious sovereign enter.

Who is this splendid ruler?
The Lord of power and might,
the conqueror of chaos.

Stretch toward heaven, you gates,
open high and wide.
Let the glorious sovereign enter.

Who is this splendid ruler?
The Lord of heaven's might,
this splendid ruler is God. □

TOBIT 13:1 – 8

Bless the Lord of justice,
who rules for ever.

Blest be the living God,
reigning for ever,
who strikes, then heals,
casts deep into the grave,
and raises up from utter ruin;
no one eludes God's hand.

Praise God, Israel,
among the nations
where you are scattered.

Announce God's greatness
wherever you are.
Extol the Lord to everyone:
the Lord is our God,
who fathered us,
God for ever.

Once God punished you
because you did wrong.
Now God comforts all of you
and gathers you from the nations
where you have been scattered.

When you turn your heart and mind
to live rightly before God,
then God will turn to you
and never hide again.

Match your praise
to all God has done for you.
Bless the Lord of justice,
who rules for ever.

Though captive, I praise the Lord.
I tell a sinful nation
how strong and great God is.

Sinners, turn back,
act justly before God,
who may yet respond
with pardon and delight.

As for me, I extol the Lord,
my heart rejoices in God Most High.
Give witness to God's glory,
in Jerusalem give praise! □

Lovers of justice, shout joy to the Lord.

Shout joy to the Lord,
lovers of justice,
how right to praise!
Praise God on the harp,
with ten-string lyre
sing to the Lord.

Sing God a new song.
Play music to match
your shout of joy.

For the word of the Lord is true:
what God says, God does.
This lover of truth and justice
fills the earth with love.

God speaks: the heavens are made;
God breathes: the stars shine.
God bottles the waters of the sea
and stores them in the deep.

All earth, be astounded,
stand in awe of God.
God speaks: the world is;
God commands: all things appear.

God blocks the plans of nations,
disrupts all they contrive.
But God's plan and design
lasts from age to age.
Blest the land whose god is the Lord,
the heirs whom God has chosen.

The Lord looks down
and sees our human kind.
From heaven God surveys
all peoples on earth.
The maker of human hearts
knows every human act.

Armies do not save kings,
brute force does not spare soldiers.
The warhorse is a sham;
despite its power, it will not save.

God keeps a loving eye
on all who believe,
on those who count on God
to bring relief from famine,
to rescue them from death.

With all we are, we wait for God,
the Lord, our help, our shield.
Our hearts find joy in the Lord;
we trust God's holy name.
Love us, Lord!
We wait for you. □

Praise the Lord, the God of Israel,
who shepherds the people and sets them free...

CANTICLE OF
ZECHARIAH

TUESDAY EVENING PRAYER

PSALM 20

God has given victory to Christ.

God defend you in battle!
set you safe above the fray!
The God of Jacob send you help,
and from holy Zion, keep you strong!

May God recall your many gifts
and be pleased with your sacrifice,
favoring all your hopes,
making your plans succeed.

Then we will sing of your conquest,
raise the flags in triumph,
to proclaim the name of our God
who grants all you ask.

Now I know for certain:
the anointed of the Lord
is given victory.
God favors him from highest heaven
with a strong, saving hand.

Some boast of chariots and horses,
but we boast of God's name.
They waver and fall,
but we stand firm.

Lord, give victory to your king,
answer us on the day we call. □

Rejoice in your victory, Lord;
we sing and praise your strength.

Lord, the king triumphs with your help,
exults in the victory you gave;
you granted what he hoped for,
accomplished what he asked.

You handed him this blessing
and crowned him with gold;
he begged only to be spared,
but you multiplied his years.

All his glory is in your victory,
for you invest him with royal splendor,
confer on him lasting blessings,
and give him joy in your presence.
The king relies on the Most High;
God's love becomes his strength.

Your hands search out your enemies,
uncover all who hate you;
you burn them with your anger,
consume them in your fiery blaze.
Your fury swallows them,
the fire devours them;
you purge them from the land
and leave them no offspring.

For they plotted and schemed against you,
but their evil did <u>not</u> succeed;
you made them turn and run
from the deadly aim <u>of</u> your arrows.
Rejoice in your vict<u>ory</u>, Lord!
We sing and <u>praise</u> your strength. □

<table>
<tr><td>REVELATION
4:11; 5:9 – 10, 12</td><td>Christ Jesus, your blood purchased for God
every tribe, language, people and nation.</td></tr>
</table>

Worthy are you, Lord God,
to receive glory, hon<u>or</u> and power,
for you are creator and <u>source</u> of all.

Worthy are y<u>ou</u>, O Christ,
to take the scroll and <u>break</u> the seals,
for you were slain,
and your blood pur<u>chased</u> for God
every tribe, language, peop<u>le</u> and nation.

You made them royal priests
to <u>serve</u> our God,
and they will <u>rule</u> on earth.

Worthy is the slaughtered Lamb,
worthy of power and wealth,
wisdom and strength,
honor and glory and praise. ☐

I acclaim the greatness of the Lord,
I delight in God my savior...

WEDNESDAY MORNING PRAYER

PSALM 36

God, you are the fount of life,
you give us light and we see.

Sin whispers with the wicked,
shares its evil, heart to heart.
These sinners shut their eyes
to all fear of God.
They refuse to see their sin,
to know it and hate it.

Their words ring false and empty,
their plans neglect what is good.
They daydream of evil,
plot their crooked ways,
seizing on all that is vile.

Your mercy, Lord, spans the sky;
your faithfulness soars among the clouds.
Your integrity towers like a mountain;
your justice runs deeper than the sea.
Lord, you embrace all life:
How we prize your tender mercy!

God, your people seek shelter,
safe in the warmth of your wings.
They feast at your full table,
slake their thirst in your cool stream,
for you are the fount of life,
you give us light and we see.

Grant mercy always to your own,
victory to honest hearts.
Keep the proud from trampling me,
assaulting me with wicked hands.
Let those sinners collapse,
struck down, never to rise. □

Grandeur and glory are yours, Lord,
with power that astonishes all.

JUDITH 16:
2 – 3a, 13 – 15

Shake tambourines! Clash cymbals!
Strike up a song to my God!
Sound a new music of praise!
Praise and call on God's name!

I sing my God a fresh new song:
"Grandeur and glory are yours, Lord,
with power that astonishes all;
no rival can match your might.

"Let all creation bend to you:
for you spoke, and they took shape;
you breathed, they came alive.
Not one can resist your voice.

"Mountain peak and ocean depth
quake to their inmost core.
Rocks melt like wax when you appear,
while you spare those who stand in awe." □

Sing out your praise to God,
to the king, sing out your praise.

All peoples, clap your hands,
shout your joy to God.
For God Most High is awesome,
great king of all the earth.

The One who conquers peoples
and sets them at our feet
chooses for beloved Jacob
a land to be our pride.

God ascends the mountain
to cheers and trumpet blasts.
Sing out your praise to God,
to the king, sing out your praise.

For God rules the earth;
sing praise with all your skill.
God rules over nations,
high on the sacred throne.

Foreign rulers join
the people of Abraham's God;
all the powers on earth
belong to God on high. □

Praise the Lord, the God of Israel,
who shepherds the people and sets them free...

WEDNESDAY EVENING PRAYER

The Lord is my saving light;
whom should I fear?

PSALM 27:1 – 6

The Lord is my saving light;
whom should I fear?
God is my fortress;
what should I dread?

When the violent come at me
to eat me alive,
a mob eager to kill —
they waver, they collapse.

Should battalions lay siege,
I will not fear;
should war rage against me,
even then I will trust.

One thing I ask the Lord,
one thing I seek:
to live in the house of God
every day of my life,
caught up in God's beauty,
at prayer in his temple.

The Lord will hide me there,
hide my life from attack:
a sheltering tent above me,
a firm rock below.

I am now beyond reach
of those who besiege me.
In his temple I will offer
a joyful sacrifice,
I will play and sing to God. □

I look for your face, O God,
I beg you not to hide.

O God, listen to me;
be gracious, answer me.
Deep within me a voice says,
"Look for the face of God!"

So I look for your face,
I beg you not to hide.
Do not shut me out in anger,
help me instead.

Do not abandon or desert me,
my savior, my God.
If my parents rejected me,
still God would take me in.

Teach me how to live,
lead me on the right road
away from my enemies.
Do not leave me to their malice;
liars breathing violence
rise to swear against me.

I know I will see
how good God is
while I am still alive.
Trust in the Lord. Be strong.
Be brave. Trust in the Lord. □

*Christ has primacy in all creation
and is in all things first.*

COLOSSIANS
1:12 – 20

Give thanks to the Father,
who made us fit
for the holy community of light
and rescued us from darkness,
bringing us into the realm
of his beloved Son
who redeemed us,
forgiving our sins.

Christ is an image
of the God we cannot see.
Christ is firstborn in all creation.

Through Christ the universe was made,
things seen and unseen,
thrones, authorities, forces, powers.
Everything was created
through Christ and for Christ.

Before anything came to be, Christ was,
and the universe is held together by Christ.

Christ is also head of the body, the church,
its beginning as firstborn from the dead
to become in all things first.

For by God's good pleasure
Christ encompasses
the full measure of power,
reconciling creation with its source
and making peace by the blood of the cross. □

I acclaim the greatness of the Lord,
I delight in God my savior...

THURSDAY MORNING PRAYER

Awake, my harp and lyre,
so I can wake up the dawn!

Care for me, God, take care of me,
I have nowhere else to hide.
Shadow me with your wings
until all danger passes.

I call to the Most High,
to God, my avenger:
send help from heaven to free me,
punish those who hound me.

Extend to me, O God,
your love that never fails,
for I find myself among lions
who crave for human flesh,
their teeth like spears and arrows,
their tongues sharp as swords.

O God, rise high above the heavens!
Spread your glory across the earth!

They rigged a net for me,
a trap to bring me down;
they dug a pit for me,
but they — they fell in!

I have decided, O God,
my decision is firm:
to you I will sing my praise.
Awake, my soul, to song!

Awake, my harp and lyre,
so I can wake up the dawn!
I will lift my voice in praise,
sing of you, Lord, to all nations.
For your love reaches heaven's edge,
your unfailing love, the skies.

O God, rise high above the heavens!
Spread your glory across the earth! □

JEREMIAH 31:
10 – 14

*God gathers the scattered flock,
guides Israel like a shepherd.*

Nations! Hear God's word,
tell your distant shores,
"God gathers the scattered flock,
guides Israel like a shepherd."

The Lord has saved Jacob's people,
loosened the enemy's grip.
They reach Zion shouting for joy,
thrilled with the goodness of God:

they see grain and oil and wine,
new lambs and young calves;
they thrive like a watered garden
never to wither again.

Young girls break into dance,
the young and old join in,
for I turn their grief to laughter,
ease their sorrow with joy.

I serve my priests rich food,
I fill my people with plenty. □

In your temple, Lord,
we recall your constant love.

Our great Lord
deserves great praise
in the city of God:

Holy mountain, beautiful height,
crown of the earth!
Zion, highest of sacred peaks,
city of the Great King!
God enthroned in its palaces
becomes our sure defense!

Watch the foreign kings
massing to attack;
seeing what they face,
they flee in terror.

Trembling grips them,
anguish like childbirth,
fury like an east wind
shattering a merchant fleet.

What we see
matches what we were told,
"This is the city the Lord protects;
our God is strong for ever."
In your temple, Lord,
we recall your constant love.

Your praise, like your name,
fills the whole world.
Your right hand holds the victory.
Mount Zion and the cities of Judah
rejoice at your justice.

March around Zion,
make the circuit,
count each tower.
Ponder these walls,
observe these citadels,

so you may tell your children:
"Here is God!
Our God for ever!
God who leads us
even against death!" □

CANTICLE OF
ZECHARIAH

Praise the Lord, the God of Israel,
who shepherds the people and sets them free…

THURSDAY EVENING PRAYER

How I begged and you healed me, God;
for ever I will thank you.

I give you high praise,
for you, Lord, raised me up
above my gloating enemy.
Lord, how I begged you,
and you, God, healed me.
You pulled me from the pit,
brought me back from Sheol.

Celebrate, all you saints,
praise this awesome God,
whose anger passes quickly,
whose mercy lasts a lifetime —
as laughter fills a day
after one brief night of tears.

When all was going well,
I thought I could never fall;
with God's powerful blessing,
I would stand like a mountain!
Then you hid your face;
I shook with fear!

I cried out, "Lord, Lord!"
I begged, I pleaded:
"What good is my blood to you?
Why push me down the pit?
Can dead bones praise you,
recount your unbroken love?
Listen to me, O God,
turn and help me now."

You changed my anguish
into this joyful dance,
pulled off my sackcloth,
gave me bright new robes,
that my life might sing your glory,
never silent in your praise.
For ever I will thank you,
O Lord my God. □

PSALM 32

Happy the pardoned,
in whom God finds no evil, no deceit.

Happy the pardoned,
whose sin is canceled,
in whom God finds
no evil, no deceit.

While I hid my sin,
my bones grew weak
from endless groaning.

Day and night,
under the weight of your hand,
my strength withered
as in a summer drought.

Then I stopped hiding my sin
and spoke out,
"God, I confess my wrong."
And you pardoned me.

No wonder the faithful
pray to you in danger!
Even a sudden flood
will never touch them.

You, my shelter,
you save me from ruin.
You encircle me
with songs of freedom.

"I show you the path to walk.
As your teacher,
I watch out for you.

"Do not be a stubborn mule,
needing bridle and bit
to be tamed."
Evil brings grief;
trusting in God brings love.

Rejoice in the Lord.
Be glad and sing,
you faithful and just. □

*God has given Christ all glory, honor and praise;
every nation shall serve him.*

We thank you, Lord,
God and ruler of all,
who is and who was.
You have claimed your power
and begun to reign.

When the nations raged
your anger stirred.
Then was the moment
to judge the dead,
to reward your servants, the prophets,
to honor your holy ones
who honored your name,
small and great alike.

Now is salvation,
the power and reign of God;
the Christ holds command.
For the one who accused the saints
day and night before God
has now been driven out.

They won the battle
by the blood of the Lamb,
and by the power of their witness
despite the threat of death.
Citizens of heaven, rejoice. □

I acclaim the greatness of the Lord,
I delight in God my savior...

CANTICLE
OF MARY

FRIDAY MORNING PRAYER

PSALM 51

In your love make Zion lovely.

Have mercy, tender God,
forget that I defied you.
Wash away my sin,
cleanse me from my guilt.

I know my evil well,
it stares me in the face,
evil done to you alone
before your very eyes.

How right your condemnation!
Your verdict clearly just.
You see me for what I am,
a sinner before my birth.

You love those centered in truth;
teach me your hidden wisdom.
Wash me with fresh water,
wash me bright as snow.

Fill me with happy songs,
let the bones you bruised now dance.
Shut your eyes to my sin,
make my guilt disappear.

Creator, reshape my heart,
God, steady my spirit.
Do not cast me aside
stripped of your holy spirit.

Save me, bring back my joy,
support me, strengthen my will.
Then I will teach your way
and sinners will turn to you.

Help me, stop my tears,
and I will sing your goodness.
Lord, give me words
and I will shout your praise.

When I offer a holocaust,
the gift does not please you.
So I offer my shattered spirit;
a changed heart you welcome.

In your love make Zion lovely,
rebuild the walls of Jerusalem.
Then sacrifice will please you,
young bulls upon your altar. □

In the Lord shall Israel triumph and glory.

ISAIAH 45:
15 – 25

You are an unseen God,
O saving God of Israel.
Makers of idols will be shamed
and paraded in disgrace.
But you, Israel, will never be shamed,
for your God upholds you for ever.

Thus says the Lord,
creator of the heavens,
God who formed the earth
and fixed it firm,
not a place of chaos,
but good to live in:
"I am the Lord.
There is no other.

"I did not speak in secret
from some dark land.
I did not say to Israel,
'Seek me in chaos.'
I am the Lord.
I speak the truth,
I say what is just.

"Gather together, you exiles,
come out from the nations
who are foolish enough
to parade their idols
and bow to gods unable to save.

"Speak out, present your case.
Consult among yourselves.
Who foretold this in ancient times?
Was it not I, the Lord?
There is no other God but me,
no God to help and deliver,
no one but me.

"Turn to me for rescue,
all you in foreign lands,
for I am God.
There is no other.

"On my word I swear:
I speak only truth
that shall not be revoked.
To me every knee shall bend,
every tongue shall swear:

"From God alone
comes victory and strength.
All who defy the Lord
shall stand in disgrace.
In the Lord shall Israel
triumph and glory." □

Serve the Lord with gladness,
enter God's presence with joy!

PSALM 100

Shout joy to the Lord, all earth,
serve the Lord with gladness,
enter God's presence with joy!

Know that the Lord is God,
our maker to whom we belong,
our shepherd, and we the flock.

Enter the temple gates,
the courtyard with thanks and praise;
give thanks and bless God's name.

Indeed the Lord is good!
God's love is for ever,
faithful from age to age. □

CANTICLE OF
ZECHARIAH

Praise the Lord, the God of Israel,
who shepherds the people and sets them free…

FRIDAY EVENING PRAYER

God, pity me, heal me for I have failed you.   PSALM 41

Blest are those ready to help the poor;
in hard times God repays their care.

God watches, protects,
blesses them in their land,
lets no enemy swallow them up!
God comforts them on their sickbed
and nurses them to health.

I said, "God, pity me,
heal me for I have failed you."
Enemies predict the worst for me:
"How soon till this one dies,
how soon forgotten?"

Visitors all wish me well,
but they come seeking bad news
to gossip on the street.

My enemies whisper
and spread the worst about me:
"Something fatal has taken hold,
this one will not get well."

Even my trusted friend
who used to eat with me
now turns on me.

Pity me, God, restore me
so I can pay them back.
Then I will know you favor me
when my foes cannot prevail.
I am innocent; uphold me!
Let me stand with you for ever.

Blessed be the Lord,
God of Israel for ever.
Amen! Amen! □

PSALM 46

The Lord of cosmic power,
Jacob's God, will shield us.

Our sure defense,
our shelter and help in trouble,
God never stands far off.

So we stand unshaken
when solid earth cracks
and volcanoes slide into the sea,
when breakers rage
and mountains tremble in the swell.

The Lord of cosmic power,
Jacob's God, will shield us.

A river delights the city of God,
home of the Holy One Most High.
With God there, the city stands;
God defends it under attack.
Nations rage, empires fall.
God speaks, earth melts.

The Lord of cosmic power,
Jacob's God, will shield us.

Come! See the wonders
God does across the earth:
everywhere stopping wars,
smashing, crushing, burning
all the weapons of war.

An end to your fighting!
Acknowledge me as God,
high over nations, high over earth.

The Lord of cosmic power,
Jacob's God, will shield us. □

All nations will gather,
bowing low to you, O God.

All you do stirs wonder,
Lord, mighty God.
Your ways are right and true,
ruler of all nations.

Who would not be moved
to glorify your name?
For you alone are holy.

All nations will gather,
bowing low to you,
for your saving works
are plainly seen. □

I acclaim the greatness of the Lord,
I delight in God my savior...

SATURDAY MORNING PRAYER

I face you in the cold night,
praying, waiting for your word.

PSALM 119:
145 – 152

My heart begs you, Lord:
hear me, so I <u>can</u> keep faith.
I beg you, make me free,
so I can <u>live</u> your laws.

I face you in the cold night
praying, waiting <u>for</u> your word.
I keep watch through the night,
repeating <u>what</u> you promise.

Hear me, loving God,
let your justice <u>make</u> me live.
The wicked close in on me;
to them your <u>law</u> is foreign.

But you, Lord, are closer still,
your law is <u>my</u> whole truth,
learned when I was young,
fixed <u>for</u> all time. □

The Lord is my strength, the Lord who saves me;
this is the God I praise.

EXODUS 15:
1 – 18

I sing of the Lord,
great <u>and</u> triumphant:
horse and rider
are cast in<u>to</u> the sea!

The Lord is my strength,
the Lord who saves me —
this is the God I praise,
the God of my ancestor.

True to the name "Lord,"
our God leads in battle,
hurls Pharaoh's chariots
and army into the sea.

The best of their warriors
sink beneath the Reed Sea,
sink like rocks to the bottom,
lie covered by the deep.

Your right arm, Lord,
is majesty and power,
your raised right arm
shatters the enemy.

Awesome your power:
you hurl down enemies,
you blaze forth in anger
to consume them like stubble.

One blast from your nostrils
and the waters pile high,
the waves pull back
to stand firm as a wall.

The enemy thinks, "Pursue them,
seize them and all they have,
feast on all their wealth,
draw the sword and destroy them."

But you send another blast;
the sea swallows them,
like lead they sink
in the terrifying waters.

Who can rival you, Lord,
among the gods?
Who can rival you,
terrifying in holiness?

Awesome this story,
fearful your wonders:
you stretched out your hand,
the earth swallowed them.

By your love you guide
this people you redeemed,
your power clears their path
to your holy place.

When nations hear, they shudder;
the Philistines writhe in fear,
all the princes of Edom
tremble in their terror,

all the chiefs of Moab
shake beyond control,
all the people of Canaan
melt away in dread.

Your mighty arm strikes terror,
they fall silent as stone,
while your people, Lord, cross over,
your own people cross over.

You brought and planted them, Lord,
on the mountain you chose,
where you make your dwelling,
the temple you built by hand.

The Lord rules for ever and ever! □

PSALM 117

Praise, give glory to God!
Nations, peoples, give glory!

Praise! Give glory to God!
Nations, peoples, give glory!

Strong the love embracing us.
Faithful the Lord for ever.

Hallelujah! □

CANTICLE OF
ZECHARIAH

Praise the Lord, the God of Israel,
who shepherds the people and sets them free…

SUNDAY
Week II

SUNDAY EVENING PRAYER I

Your word is a lamp for my steps,
a light for my path, hallelujah.

Your word is a lamp for my steps,
a light for my path.
I have sworn firmly
to uphold your just rulings.

I have suffered so much,
give me the life you promise.
Receive, Lord, all that I say,
and teach me your wisdom.

Though danger stalks,
I will never forget your law.
Though the wicked set traps,
I will not stray from you.

Your laws are my heritage,
the joy of my heart for ever.
I am determined to obey
for a lasting reward. □

You show me the road to life:
boundless joy at your side for ever, hallelujah.

Protect me, God,
I turn to you for help.
I profess, "You are my Lord,
my greatest good."

I once put faith in false gods,
the idols of the land.
Now I make no offering to them,
nor invoke their names.
Those who chase after them
add grief upon grief.

Lord, you measure out my portion,
the shape of my future;
you mark off the best place for me
to enjoy my inheritance.

I bless God who teaches me,
who schools my heart even at night.
I am sure God is here,
right beside me.
I cannot be shaken.

So my heart rejoices,
my body thrills with life,
my whole being rests secure.

You will not abandon me to Sheol,
nor send your faithful one to death.
You show me the road to life:
boundless joy at your side for ever! □

*At the name of Jesus every knee will bend
in heaven and on earth.*

Though in the form of God,
Jesus did not claim
equality with God
but emptied himself,
taking the form of a slave,
human like one of us.

Flesh and blood,
he humbled himself,
obeying to the death,
death on a cross.
For this very reason
God lifted him high
and gave him the name
above all names.

So at the name of Jesus
every knee will bend
in heaven, on earth,
and in the world below,
and every tongue exclaim
to the glory of God the Father,
"Jesus Christ is Lord." □

I acclaim the greatness of the Lord,
I delight in God my savior...

SUNDAY MORNING PRAYER

Blest is the one who comes,
who comes in the name of the Lord, hallelujah.

Give thanks, the Lord is good,
God's love is for ever!
Now let Israel say,
"God's love is for ever!"

Let the house of Aaron say,
"God's love is for ever!"
Let all who revere the Lord say,
"God's love is for ever!"

In distress I called to the Lord,
who answered and set me free.
The Lord is with me, I fear not.
What can they do to me?
The Lord my help is with me,
I can face my foes.

Better to trust in the Lord
than rely on human help.
Better to trust in the Lord
than rely on generous hearts.

The nations surrounded me;
in God's name, I will crush them!
Surrounded me completely;
in God's name, I will crush them!
Surrounded me like bees,
blazed like brushwood fire;
in God's name, I will crush them!

I was pushed to falling,
but the Lord gave me help.
My strength, my song is the Lord,
who has become my savior.

Glad songs of victory sound
within the tents of the just.
With right hand raised high,
the Lord strikes with force.

I shall not die but live
to tell the Lord's great deeds.
The Lord punished me severely,
but did not let me die.

Open the gates of justice,
let me praise God within them.
This is the Lord's own gate,
only the just will enter.
I thank you for you answered me,
and you became my savior.

The stone the builders rejected
has become the cornerstone.
This is the work of the Lord,
how wonderful in our eyes.

This is the day the Lord made,
let us rejoice and be glad.
Lord, give us the victory!
Lord, grant us success!

Blest is the one who comes,
who comes in the name of the Lord.
We bless you from the Lord's house.
The Lord God is our light:
adorn the altar with branches.

I will thank you, my God,
I will praise you highly.
Give thanks, the Lord is good,
God's love is for ever! □

Sing a hymn of praise to our God, hallelujah.

DANIEL 3:
52 – 57

Blest are you, God of our ancestors,
praised and lifted above all for ever!
Blest your holy name, full of wonder,
praised and lifted above all for ever!

Blest are you in your temple of glory,
acclaimed and honored for ever.
Blest are you who see the depths
from the cherubim throne,
praised and lifted above all for ever!

Blest are you enthroned in majesty,
praised and lifted above all for ever!
Blest are you beyond the stars,
acclaimed and honored for ever!

All you creatures, bless our God,
acclaimed and exalted for ever! □

Praise! Praise God's mighty deeds
and noble majesty, hallelujah!

Praise! Praise God in the temple,
in the highest heavens!
Praise! Praise God's mighty deeds
and noble majesty.

Praise! Praise God with trumpet blasts,
with lute and harp.
Praise! Praise God with timbrel and dance,
with strings and pipes.

Praise! Praise God with crashing cymbals,
with ringing cymbals.
All that is alive, praise. Praise the Lord.
Hallelujah! □

Praise the Lord, the God of Israel,
who shepherds the people and sets them free...

SUNDAY EVENING PRAYER II

*Christ the Lord is priest
and king for ever, hallelujah.*

The Lord decrees to the king:
"Take the throne at my right hand,
I will make your enemies a footrest.
I will raise your scepter
over Zion and beyond,
over all your enemies.

"Your people stand behind you
on the day you take command.
You are made holy, splendid,
newborn like the dawn,
fresh like the dew."

God's oath is firm:
"You are a priest for ever,
the rightful king by my decree."
The Lord stands at your side
to destroy kings
on the day of wrath.

God executes judgment,
crushes the heads of nations,
and brings carnage worldwide.
The victor drinks
from a wayside stream
and rises refreshed. □

God will bless all believers,
the small and the great, hallelujah.

Not to us, Lord, not to us,
but to your name give glory,
because of your love,
because of your truth.

Why do the nations say,
"Where is their God?"
Our God is in the heavens
and answers to no one.

Their gods are crafted by hand,
mere silver and gold,
with mouths that are mute
and eyes that are blind,
with ears that are deaf
and noses that cannot smell.

Their hands cannot feel,
their feet cannot walk,
their throats are silent.
Their makers, their worshipers
will be just like them.

Let Israel trust God,
their help and shield.
Let the house of Aaron trust God,
their help and shield.
Let all believers trust God,
their help and shield.

The Lord has remembered us
and will bless us,
will bless the house of Israel,
will bless the house of Aaron.
God will bless all believers,
the small and the great.

May God bless you more and more,
bless all your children.
May you truly be blessed
by the maker of heaven and earth.

To the Lord belong the heavens,
to us the earth below!
The dead sing no Hallelujah,
nor do those in the silent ground.
But we will bless you, Lord,
now and for ever.

Hallelujah! □

Praise our God, you faithful servants!
In awe praise God, alleluia!

Alleluia! (*or:* Amen. Alleluia!)
Salvation, glory and power to God!
Alleluia, Alleluia!
Right and sure, the judgments of God!
Alleluia, Alleluia!

REVELATION
19:1 – 7

Outside Lent

Alleluia!
Praise our God, you faithful servants!
Alleluia, Alleluia!
In awe praise God, you small and great!
Alleluia, Alleluia!

Alleluia!
The Lord God almighty rules!
Alleluia, Alleluia!
Be glad, rejoice, give glory to God!
Alleluia, Alleluia!

Alleluia!
The wedding feast of the Lamb begins.
Alleluia, Alleluia!
The bride is radiant, clothed in glory.
Alleluia, Alleluia! (*or:* Amen. Alleluia!) □

1 PETER 2: 21 – 24	*Christ carried our sins*
In Lent	*in his body to the cross,*

Christ carried our sins
in his body to the cross,
that we might die to sin
and live for justice.

Christ suffered for us
leaving us an example,
that we might walk
in his footsteps.

He did nothing wrong;
no false word
ever passed his lips.

When they cursed him
he returned no curse.
Tortured, he made no threats
but trusted in the perfect judge.

He carried our sins
in his body
to the cross,
that we might die to sin
and live for justice.
When he was wounded,
we were healed. ☐

I acclaim the greatness of the Lord,
I delight in God my savior...

CANTICLE
OF MARY

PSALM 42

I thirst for God, the living stream.
When will I see God's face?

As a deer craves running water,
I thirst for you, my God;
I thirst for God,
the living God.
When will I see your face?

Tears are my steady diet.
Day and night I hear,
"Where is your God?"

I cry my heart out,
I remember better days:
when I entered the house of God,
I was caught in the joyful sound
of pilgrims giving thanks.

Why are you sad, my heart?
Why do you grieve?
Wait for the Lord.
I will yet praise God my savior.

My heart is sad.
Even from Jordan and Hermon,
from the peak of Mizar,
I remember you.

There the deep roars to deep;
your torrents crash over me.
The love God summoned by day
sustained my praise by night,
my prayer to the living God.

I complain to God,
who I thought was rock:
"Why have you forgotten me?
Why am I bent double
under the weight of enemies?

"Their insults grind me to dust.
Day and night they say,
'Where is your God?'"

Why are you sad, my heart?
Why do you grieve?
Wait for the Lord.
I will yet praise God my savior. □

Show us the radiance of your mercy, God.

SIRACH 36:
1 – 7, 13, 16 – 22

Show us mercy, God of all,
teach every land to fear you.
Strike boldly against the enemy,
display your power.

Make them an example of your glory,
as we once showed them your holiness.
Then they will know what we know:
there is no God but you.
Forge new signs, new wonders
with your strong right hand.

Gather every tribe of Jacob
to reclaim its birthright.
Be kind to Israel, your firstborn,
to the people who bear your name.

Deal gently with Jerusalem,
your holy city,
where your throne is fixed.
Fill Zion with your splendor,
your temple with your glory.

Make real the vision
prophets spoke in your name;
keep faith with what you began.
Reward those who hope in you,
prove the prophets right.

Answer the pleas of the faithful
and favor us as always.
Then the world will know
that you are God for ever. □

PSALM 19:2 – 7   *The sky tells the glory of God.*

The sky tells the glory of God,
tells the genius of God's work.
Day carries the news to day,
night brings the message to night,

without a word, without a sound,
without a voice being heard,
yet their message fills the world,
their news reaches its rim.

There God has pitched a tent
for the sun to rest and rise renewed
like a bridegroom rising from bed,
an athlete eager to run the race.

It springs from the edge of the earth,
runs a course across the sky
to win the race at heaven's end.
Nothing on earth escapes its heat. □

Praise the Lord, the God of Israel,
who shepherds the people and sets them free...

CANTICLE OF
ZECHARIAH

MONDAY EVENING PRAYER

PSALM 45:2 – 10   *Unrivaled in beauty, gracious in speech:*
how God has blessed you!

A great song fills my heart,
I will recite it to the king,
my tongue as skilled as the scribal pen.

Unrivaled in beauty,
gracious in speech —
how God has blessed you!

Hero, take up your sword,
majestic in your armor.
Ride on for truth,
show justice to the poor,
wield your power boldly.

Your weapons are ready;
nations fall beneath your might,
your enemies lose heart.

Your throne is as lasting
as the everlasting God.
Integrity is the law of your land.

Because you love justice and hate evil,
God, your God, anoints you
above your peers with festive oil.

Your clothes are fragrant
with myrrh and aloes
and cinnamon flowers.
Music of strings welcomes you
to the ivory palace
and lifts your heart.

Royal women honor you.
On your right hand the queen,
wearing gold of Ophir. □

The bridegroom is here;
go out to welcome him.

PSALM 45:
11 – 18

Mark these words, daughter:
leave your family behind,
forget your father's house.

The king desires your beauty.
He is your lord.
Tyre comes with gifts,
the wealthy honor you.

The robes of the queen
are embroidered with gold.
In brilliant attire
she is led to the king;
her attendants follow.
In high spirits
they enter the royal palace.

Your sons will inherit
the throne your fathers held.
They shall reign throughout the land.

Every age will recall your name.
This song will fix it in their memory. □

EPHESIANS 1:
3 – 10

In the fullness of time
God planned to unite the entire universe
through Christ.

Bless God, the Father of our Lord Jesus Christ,
who blessed us from heaven through Christ
with every blessing of the Spirit.

Before laying the world's foundation,
God chose us in Christ
to live a pure and holy life.

God determined out of love
to adopt us through Jesus Christ
for the praise and glory of that grace
granted us in the Beloved.

By Christ's blood we were redeemed,
our sins forgiven
through extravagant love.

With perfect wisdom and insight
God freely displayed the mystery
of what was always intended:
a plan for the fullness of time
to unite the entire universe through Christ. □

I acclaim the greatness of the Lord,
I delight in God my savior...

CANTICLE
OF MARY

TUESDAY MORNING PRAYER

Send your light and truth, my God.

Decide in my favor, God,
plead my case against the hateful,
defend me from liars and thugs.
For you are God my fortress.

Why have you forgotten me?
Why am I bent double
under the weight of enemies?

Send your light and truth.
They will escort me
to the holy mountain
where you make your home.

I will approach the altar of God,
God, my highest joy,
and praise you with the harp,
God, my God.

Why are you sad, my heart?
Why do you grieve?
Wait for the Lord.
I will yet praise God my savior. □

We will sing to God our savior
as long as we live.

ISAIAH 38:
10 – 14, 17 – 20

In the prime of my life
I felt death reaching for me,
calling me to Sheol's gates,
cutting short my days.

I was stunned to think
I will never again see God,
never again see a human face
here on this earth.

My life collapsed
like a tent pulled down,
like cloth cut from a loom
before it is finished.
Day and night I faced death.

God like a lion
tears my bones apart.
I groan until dawn.
Day and night I face death.

Shrill as a crane,
mournful as a dove,
I weep before heaven,
"My world is collapsing;
Lord, hold me up."

You brought good from my pain.
You cast aside my sins
and from the deadly pit
snatched me away.

Who thanks you in the grave?
Death does not praise you.
The dead in Sheol
no longer hope in you.

Only those alive,
alive like me,
can thank you
and tell their children
how faithful you are.

The Lord saved me.
Let us make music
and sing in the temple
as long as we live. □

PSALM 65

All praise is yours, God in Zion.

Praise is yours, God in Zion.
Now is the moment
to keep our vow,
for you, God, are listening.

All people come to you
bringing their shameful deeds.
You free us from guilt,
from overwhelming sin.

Happy are those you invite
and then welcome to your courts.
Fill us with the plenty of your house,
the holiness of your temple.

You give victory
in answer to our prayer.
You inspire awe, God, our savior,
hope of distant lands and waters.

Clothed in power,
you steady the mountains;
you still the roaring seas,
restless waves, raging nations.
People everywhere
stand amazed at what you do,
east and west shout for joy.

You tend and water the land.
How wonderful the harvest!
You fill your springs,
ready the seeds, prepare the grain.

You soak the furrows
and level the ridges.
With softening rain
you bless the land with growth.

You crown the year with riches.
All you touch comes alive:
untilled lands yield crops,
hills are dressed in joy,

flocks clothe the pastures,
valleys wrap themselves in grain.
They all shout for joy
and break into song. □

CANTICLE OF
ZECHARIAH

Praise the Lord, the God of Israel,
who shepherds the people and sets them free…

TUESDAY EVENING PRAYER

We cannot save ourselves,
but God will rescue us.

PSALM 49:2 – 13

Everyone, take heed,
all the world, listen,
high and low,
rich and poor alike.

I have wisdom you need to hear.
I see to the heart of things.
I tune my ear to the truth
and set my insight to music.

Why should I be afraid in bad times
when enemies surround me,
disdainful in their power,
arrogant in their wealth?

We cannot save ourselves,
cannot set things right with God;
the price is too high,
well beyond our means.

There is no escaping death,
no avoiding the grave.
Look, even the wisest die.
Fools and idiots perish with them,
and others claim their wealth.

The grave is the only home
where they settle for good,
even if their land
still bears their name.

No matter how great,
no one sees the truth:
we die like beasts. □

I know God will rescue me
and save me from the grip of death.

Here is the fate of those
only concerned for themselves:
they go straight to Sheol.

Death shepherds them
right into the grave,
where flesh is eaten up
and earth consumes them.

But I know God will rescue me,
save me from the grip of death.

Do not worry about wealth,
when someone else becomes rich.
You cannot take it to your grave,
wealth is worth nothing in death.

No matter how wealthy,
no matter how many tell you,
"My, how well you have done,"
the rich all join the dead
never to see light again.

No matter how great,
no one sees the truth:
we die like beasts. □

Worthy is the slaughtered Lamb,
worthy of honor and glory and praise.

REVELATION
4:11; 5:9 – 10, 12

Worthy are you, Lord God,
to receive glory, honor and power,
for you are creator and source of all.

Worthy are you, O Christ,
to take the scroll and break the seals,
for you were slain,
and your blood purchased for God
every tribe, language, people and nation.

You made them royal priests,
to serve our God,
and they will rule on earth.

Worthy is the slaughtered Lamb,
worthy of power and wealth,
wisdom and strength,
honor and glory and praise. □

I acclaim the greatness of the Lord,
I delight in God my savior ...

CANTICLE
OF MARY

WEDNESDAY MORNING PRAYER

God, you alone are holy.
What god compares to you?

I cry to you, God! I plead with you!
If only you would hear me!

By day I seek you in my distress,
by night I raise my hands in prayer,
but my spirit refuses comfort.
I groan when I remember you;
when I think of you, I grow faint.

You keep me from sleep.
Troubled, I cannot speak.
I consider former days,
the years gone by;
all night, memories fill my heart,
I brood and question.

Will God always reject me?
Never again be pleased?
Has God stopped loving me
and cut me off for ever?
Can God forget to pity,
can anger block God's mercy?

It troubles me to think
the Almighty has grown weak.
I recall your awesome deeds,
your wonders of old.
I reflect on all you have done,
on all your works.

You alone are holy.
What god compares to you?
You are the God of power,
strong among the nations.
You reached out to save your people,
the children of Jacob and Joseph.

Seeing you, the waters churned,
shuddering, writhing,
convulsed to the depths.
Clouds poured down rain,
thunder shook the heavens,
lightning darted like arrows.

And the thunder rolled,
flashes lit up the world,
the earth trembled and quaked.
You set a path through the sea,
a way through raging waters,
with no trace of your footprints.

You led your flock
under Moses and Aaron. □

I acclaim the greatness of God,
who casts down the mighty and lifts up the poor.

I acclaim the Lord's greatness,
source of my strength.
I devour my foe,
I say to God with joy:
"You saved my life.
Only you are holy, Lord;
there is none but you,
no other rock like you."

God knows when deeds match words,
so make no arrogant claims.
The weapons of the strong are broken,
the defenseless gain strength.
The overfed now toil to eat,
while the hungry have their fill.

The childless bear many children,
but the fertile learn they are sterile.
The Lord commands death and life,
consigns to Sheol or raises up.

God deals out poverty and wealth,
casts down and lifts up,
raising the poor from squalor,
the needy from the trash heap,
to sit with the high and mighty,
taking their places of honor.

God owns the universe
and sets the earth within it.
God walks with the faithful
but silences the wicked in darkness;
their power does not prevail.

God's enemies will be broken,
heaven thunders against them.
The Lord will judge the earth,
and give power to the king,
victory to the anointed. □

The Lord rules:
joy touches distant lands.

PSALM 97

The Lord rules: the earth is eager,
joy touches distant lands.
God is wrapped in thunder cloud,
throned on justice, throned on right.

Fire marches out in front
and burns up all resistance.
Overhead, God's lightning flares,
the earth shudders to see it.

Mountains melt down like wax
before the Lord, the ruler of all.
Overhead God's justice resounds,
a glory all people can see.

Idolators are the fools,
they brag of empty gods.
You gods, be subject to the Lord!
Zion hears, and is happy.
The cities of Judah are joyful
about your judgments, Lord.

You, Lord, you reach high
in majesty above the earth,
far higher than any god.
Those who love the Lord hate evil;
God shields their faithful lives
and breaks the hold of the wicked.

Light will rain down on the just,
joy on the loyal heart.
Be joyous in the Lord God,
you people of faith,
praise God's holy name! □

CANTICLE OF
ZECHARIAH

Praise the Lord, the God of Israel,
who shepherds the people and sets them free…

WEDNESDAY EVENING PRAYER

Wait, my soul, silent for God,
for God alone, my hope.

PSALM 62

My soul waits, silent for God,
for God alone, my salvation,
alone my rock, my safety,
my refuge: I stand secure.

How long will some of you attack
tearing others down
as if walls or fences
on the verge of collapse?

You scheme to topple them,
so smug in your lies;
your lips are all blessing,
but murder fills your heart.

Wait, my soul, silent for God,
for God alone, my hope,
alone my rock, my safety,
my refuge: I stand secure.

God is my glory and safety,
my stronghold, my haven.
People, give your hearts to God,
trust always! God is our haven.

Mortals are but a breath,
nothing more than a mirage;
set them on the scales,
they prove lighter than mist.

Avoid extortion and fraud,
the hopes they breed are nothing;
and if you should grow rich,
place no trust in wealth.

Time and again God said,
"Strength and love are mine to give."
The Lord repays us all
in light of what we do. □

Favor and bless us, Lord.
Let your face shine on us.

Favor and bless us, Lord.
Let your face shine on us,
revealing your way to all peoples,
salvation the world over.

Let nations sing your praise,
every nation on earth.

The world will shout for joy,
for you rule the planet with justice.
In fairness you govern the nations
and guide the peoples of earth.

Let the nations sing your praise,
every nation on earth.

The land delivers its harvest,
God, our God, has blessed us.
O God, continue your blessing,
may the whole world worship you. □

Through Christ the universe was made,
things seen and unseen.

COLOSSIANS
1:12 – 20

Give thanks to the Father,
who made us fit
for the holy community of light
and rescued us from darkness,
bringing us into the realm
of his beloved Son
who redeemed us,
forgiving our sins.

Christ is an image
of the God we cannot see.
Christ is firstborn in all creation.

Through Christ the universe was made,
things seen and unseen,
thrones, authorities, forces, powers.
Everything was created
through Christ and for Christ.

Before anything came to be, Christ was,
and the universe is held together by Christ.

Christ is also head of the body, the church,
its beginning as firstborn from the dead
to become in all things first.

For by God's good pleasure
Christ encompasses
the full measure of power,
reconciling creation with its source
and making peace by the blood of the cross. □

I acclaim the greatness of the Lord,
I delight in God my savior...

THURSDAY MORNING PRAYER

Gather your strength, O God,
come, save us, Shepherd of Israel.

Hear us, Shepherd of Israel,
leader of Joseph's flock.
From your throne on the cherubim
shine out for Ephraim,
for Benjamin and Manasseh.
Gather your strength,
come, save us!

Restore to us, God,
the light of your presence,
and we shall be saved.

How long, Lord God of might,
will you smoulder with rage,
despite our prayers?

For bread you feed us tears,
we drink them by the barrel.
You let our neighbors mock,
our enemies scorn us.

Restore to us, God of might,
the light of your presence,
and we shall be saved.

You brought a vine from Egypt,
cleared out nations to plant it;
you prepared the ground
and made it take root
to fill the land.

It overshadowed the mountains,
towered over the mighty cedars,
stretched its branches to the sea,
its roots to the distant river.

Why have you now torn down its walls?
All who pass by steal the grapes,
wild boars tear up its roots,
beasts devour its fruit.

Turn our way, God of might,
look down from heaven;
tend this vine you planted,
cherish it once more.
May those who slashed and burned it
wither at your rebuke.

Rest your hand upon your chosen one
who draws strength from you.
We have not turned from you.
Give us life again
and we will invoke your name.

Restore to us, Lord God of might,
the light of your presence,
and we shall be saved. □

Praise the Lord! proclaim God's Name!

I praise you, Lord!
When your rage turned on me,
you turned it away
and now you console me.

God is my savior,
my trust knows no fear;
God's strength is my strength,
yes, God is my savior.

With joy you will draw water
from God's saving well;
then you will say to each other,
"Praise the Lord! proclaim God's name!"

Tell the world what God does,
make known this majestic name.
Sing the wonders God works,
recount them in every land.

Shout and sing for joy,
citizens of Zion,
for great among you
is the Holy One of Israel! □

Shout joy to God, the God of our strength.

Shout joy to God,
the God of our strength,
sing to the God of Jacob.

Lift hearts, strike tambourines,
sound lyre and harp.
Blow trumpets at the New Moon,
till the full moon of our feast.

For this is a law for Israel,
the command of Jacob's God,
decreed for the house of Joseph
when we marched from Egypt.

We heard a voice unknown:
"I lifted burdens from your backs,
a blistering load from your hands.

"You cried out in pain
and I rescued you;
robed in thunder,
I answered you.
At the waters of Meribah
I tested you.

"My people, hear my complaint;
Israel, if you would only listen.
You shall have no other gods,
do not bow before them.
I am the Lord your God.
I brought you out of Egypt
and fed your hungry mouths.

"But you would not hear me,
my people rejected me.
So I hardened your hearts,
and you left me out of your plans.
My people, if you would only listen!
Israel, walk in my ways!

"Then I will strike your enemy,
and put them all to flight.
With their fate sealed,
my foes will grovel at your feet.
But you, O Israel,
will feast on finest wheat,
will savor pure wild honey." □

Praise the Lord, the God of Israel,
who shepherds the people and sets them free...

CANTICLE OF
ZECHARIAH

THURSDAY EVENING PRAYER

PSALM 72:
1 – 11

I have made you the light of all nations
to carry my salvation to the ends of the earth.

God, give your king judgment,
the son of the king
your sense of what is right;
help him judge your people
and do right for the powerless.

May mountains bear peace,
hills bring forth justice.
May the king defend the poor,
set their children free,
and kill their oppressors.

May he live as long as the sun,
as long as the moon, for ever.
May he be like rain on a field,
like showers that soak the earth.

May justice sprout in his time,
peace till the moon is no more.
May he rule from sea to sea,
from the River to the ends of the earth.

Enemies will cower before him,
they will lick the dust.
Kings from Tarshish and the islands
will bring their riches to him.

Kings of Sheba, kings of Saba
will carry gifts to him.
All kings will bow before him,
all the nations serve him. □

The king will rescue the poor,
will save their lives from violence.

He will rescue the poor at their call,
those no one speaks for.
Those no one cares for
he hears and will save,
save their lives from violence,
lives precious in his eyes.

Every day they pray for him
and bless him all his life.
Long life to him!
Gold to him from Saba!

May wheat be thick in the fields,
fruit trees sway on the slope.
May cities teem with people,
thick as the forests of Lebanon.

May his name live on for ever,
live as long as the sun.
May all find blessing in him,
and he be blest by all.

Blessed be Israel's God,
Lord of wonderful deeds!
Bless God's name for ever!
Let God's glory fill the world!
Amen and Amen! □

Now is salvation,
the power and reign of God.

We thank you, Lord,
God and ruler of all,
who is and who was.
You have claimed your power
and begun to reign.

When the nations raged
your anger stirred.
Then was the moment
to judge the dead,
to reward your servants, the prophets,
to honor your holy ones
who honored your name,
small and great alike.

Now is salvation,
the power and reign of God;
the Christ holds command.
For the one who accused the saints
day and night before God
has now been driven out.

They won the battle
by the blood of the Lamb,
and by the power of their witness
despite the threat of death.
Citizens of heaven, rejoice. □

I acclaim the greatness of the Lord,
I delight in God my savior...

CANTICLE
OF MARY

FRIDAY MORNING PRAYER

You welcome a changed heart, O God.

Have mercy, tender God,
forget that I defied you.
Wash away my sin,
cleanse me from my guilt.

I know my evil well,
it stares me in the face,
evil done to you alone
before your very eyes.

How right your condemnation!
Your verdict clearly just.
You see me for what I am,
a sinner before my birth.

You love those centered in truth;
teach me your hidden wisdom.
Wash me with fresh water,
wash me bright as snow.

Fill me with happy songs,
let the bones you bruised now dance.
Shut your eyes to my sin,
make my guilt disappear.

Creator, reshape my heart,
God, steady my spirit.
Do not cast me aside
stripped of your holy spirit.

Save me, bring back my joy,
support me, strengthen my will.
Then I will teach your way
and sinners will turn to you.

Help me, stop my tears,
and I will sing your goodness.
Lord, give me words
and I will shout your praise.

When I offer a holocaust,
the gift does not please you.
So I offer my shattered spirit;
a changed heart you welcome.

In your love make Zion lovely,
rebuild the walls of Jerusalem.
Then sacrifice will please you,
young bulls upon your altar. □

Act quickly for us,
not in anger but with compassion.

HABAKKUK 3:
2 – 4, 13a,
15 – 19

They told me what you did, O Lord;
I listened, struck with awe.
Show your strength again,
act quickly for us,
not in anger but with compassion.

Now God comes from distant Teman,
the Holy One from Mount Paran.
God's brilliance fills the skies,
its grandeur lights the earth.
It blazes with a blinding flame
that conceals God's might.

You rise to save your people,
to rescue your anointed.
You ride your horses through the sea
and make the oceans rage.

I shake at their roar,
my stomach churns, my voice fails,
my knees buckle, I fall!
I wait for the day of agony
to overwhelm my foes.

Even if the fig tree fails
and vines bear no fruit,
if olives yield no oil
and fields no grain,
if sheep stray from their pens
and cattle from their stalls,
still I will glorify the Lord,
still rejoice in God my savior!

The Lord, my strength,
lets me run like a stag
and leap the highest mountain. □

Jerusalem, give glory to God!

Jerusalem, give glory!
Praise God with song, O Zion!
For the Lord strengthens your gates
guarding your children within.
The Lord fills your land with peace,
giving you golden wheat.

God speaks to the earth,
the word speeds forth.
The Lord sends heavy snow
and scatters frost like ashes.

The Lord hurls chunks of hail.
Who can stand such cold?
God speaks, the ice melts;
God breathes, the streams flow.

God speaks his word to Jacob,
to Israel, his laws and decrees.
God has not done this for others,
no others receive this wisdom.

Hallelujah! □

Praise the Lord, the God of Israel,
who shepherds the people and sets them free…

FRIDAY EVENING PRAYER

PSALM 116:1 – 9

God rescues me from death,
steadying my feet.

I am filled with love,
for the Lord hears me;
the Lord bends to my voice
whenever I call.

Death had me in its grip,
the grave's trap was set,
grief held me fast.
I cried out for God,
"Please, Lord, rescue me!"

Kind and faithful is the Lord,
gentle is our God.
The Lord shelters the poor,
raises me from the dust.
Rest once more, my heart,
for you know the Lord's love.

God rescues me from death,
wiping my tears,
steadying my feet.
I walk with the Lord
in this land of the living. □

My help is the Lord,
who made earth and the heavens.

If I look to the mountains,
will they come to my aid?
My help is the Lord,
who made earth and the heavens.

May God, ever wakeful,
keep you from stumbling;
the guardian of Israel
neither rests nor sleeps.

God shields you,
a protector by your side.
The sun shall not harm you by day
nor the moon at night.

God shelters you from evil,
securing your life.
God watches over you near and far,
now and always. □

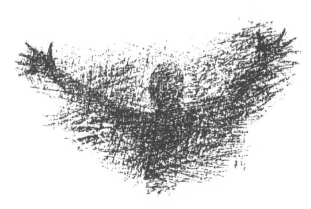

Your ways are right and true,
ruler of all nations.

All you do stirs wonder,
Lord, mighty God.
Your ways are right and true,
ruler of all nations.

Who would not be moved
to glorify your name?
For you alone are holy.

All nations will gather,
bowing low to you,
for your saving works
are plainly seen. □

I acclaim the greatness of the Lord,
I delight in God my savior...

SATURDAY MORNING PRAYER

How good to sing your love at dawn,
your faithfulness at dusk.

How good to thank you, Lord,
to praise your name, Most High,
to sing your love at dawn,
your faithfulness at dusk
with sound of lyre and harp,
with music of the lute.
For your work brings delight,
your deeds invite song.

I marvel at what you do.
Lord, how deep your thought!
Fools do not grasp this,
nor the senseless understand.
Scoundrels spring up like grass,
flourish and quickly wither.
You, Lord, stand firm for ever.

See how your enemies perish,
scattered to the winds,
while you give me brute strength,
pouring rich oil upon me.
I have faced my enemies,
heard them plot against me.

The just grow tall like palm trees,
majestic like cedars of Lebanon.
They are planted in the temple courts
and flourish in God's house,
green and heavy with fruit
even in old age.

Proclaim that God is just,
my rock without a fault. □

DEUTERONOMY
32:1 – 12

I will praise the Lord's name,
I will tell of God's greatness.

Hear me, heaven and earth,
listen to what I say.
May my thoughts fall like rain,
may my words cling like dew,
like gentle rain upon tender grass,
like showers upon seedlings.
I will praise the Lord's name,
I will tell of God's greatness.

God is the rock,
whose works are perfect,
whose ways are right,
a God faithful and true,
just and without deceit.

But the corrupt and headstrong
treat God with contempt,
they are no longer God's children.

Is this how you thank God,
you slow-witted fools?
Did God not father you,
create you, and provide for you?

Remember ancient times,
think back to ages past.
Ask your parents; they will tell you,
your elders will teach you.

When God gave the nations their land,
dividing the human race,
the Most High set boundaries for peoples,
equal to the number of gods.

The Lord adopted Jacob,
claimed Israel as a people,
finding them in the wilderness,
in the wild and howling wasteland,
enfolding them with care,
keeping a loving eye on them.

Like an eagle rousing its young,
hovering over its little ones,
spreading its wings to carry them,
to bear them up in flight,
the Lord alone guided Israel;
there is no other God. □

*Lord our God, the whole world tells
the greatness of your name.*

Lord our God,
the whole world tells
the greatness of your name.
Your glory reaches
beyond the stars.

Even the babble of infants
declares your strength,
your power to halt
the enemy and avenger.

I see your handiwork
in the heavens:
the moon and the stars
you set in place.

What is humankind
that you remember them,
the human race
that you care for them?

You treat them like gods,
dressing them in glory and splendor.
You give them charge of the earth,
laying all at their feet:

cattle and sheep,
wild beasts,
birds of the sky,
fish of the sea,
every swimming creature.

Lord our God,
the whole world tells
the greatness of your name. □

Praise the Lord, the God of Israel,
who shepherds the people and sets them free…

CANTICLE OF
ZECHARIAH

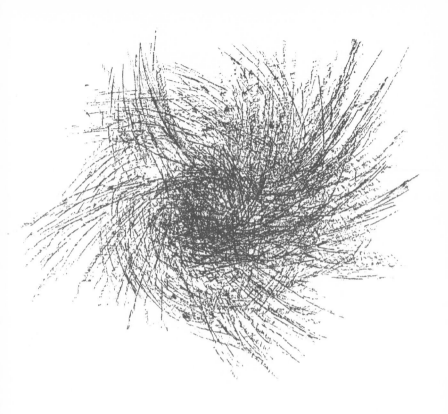

SUNDAY
Week III

PSALM 113

*Praise the Lord's name here and in every place,
from east to west.*

Servants of God, praise,
praise the name of the Lord.
Bless the Lord's name
now and always.
Praise the Lord's name
here and in every place,
from east to west.

The Lord towers above nations,
God's glory shines over the heavens.
Who compares to our God?
Who is enthroned so high?

The Lord bends down
to see heaven and earth,
to raise the weak from the dust
and lift the poor from the mire,
to seat them with princes
in the company of their leaders.

The childless, no longer alone,
rejoice now in many children.

Hallelujah! □

I raise the cup of freedom
as I call on God's name.

I believe, even as I say,
"I am afflicted."
I believe, even though I scream,
"Everyone lies!"

What gift can ever repay
God's gift to me?
I raise the cup of freedom
as I call on God's name!
I fulfill my vows to you, Lord,
standing before your assembly.

Lord, you hate to see
your faithful ones die.
I beg you, Lord, hear me:
it is I, the servant you love,
I, the child of your servant.
You freed me from death's grip.

I bring a gift of thanks,
as I call on your name.
I fulfill my vows to you, Lord,
standing before your assembly,
in the courts of your house,
within the heart of Jerusalem.

Hallelujah! □

*Jesus humbled himself
and God lifted him high.*

Though in the form of God,
Jesus did not claim
equality with God
but emptied himself,
taking the form of a slave,
human like one of us.

Flesh and blood,
he humbled himself,
obeying to the death,
death on a cross.
For this very reason
God lifted him high
and gave him the name
above all names.

So at the name of Jesus
every knee will bend
in heaven, on earth,
and in the world below,
and every tongue exclaim
to the glory of God the Father,
"Jesus Christ is Lord." □

CANTICLE
OF MARY

I acclaim the greatness of the Lord,
I delight in God my savior…

SUNDAY MORNING PRAYER I

High above ocean breakers,
you, God, rise with might.

PSALM 93

Lord, you reign with glory,
draped in splendor, girt with power.
The world stands firm,
not to be shaken,
for your throne, ageless God,
has stood from of old.

Onward roll the waves, O God,
onward like thunder,
onward like fury.
Thundering above the waters,
high above ocean breakers,
you, God, rise with might.

Your decrees stand unshaken;
the beauty of holiness
fills you for ever, Lord. □

Bless God, heaven and earth.
Give praise and glory for ever.

DANIEL 3:
56 – 88

Bless God beyond the stars.
Give praise and glory.
Bless God, heaven and earth.
Give praise and glory for ever.

Bless God, angels of God.
Give praise and glory.
Bless God, highest heavens.
Give praise and glory.

Bless God, waters above.
Give praise and glory.
Bless God, spirits of God.
Give praise and glory.

Bless God, sun and moon.
Give praise and glory.
Bless God, stars of heaven.
Give praise and glory for ever.

Bless God, rainstorm and dew.
Give praise and glory.
Bless God, gales and winds.
Give praise and glory.

Bless God, fire and heat.
Give praise and glory.
Bless God, frost and cold.
Give praise and glory.

Bless God, dew and snow.
Give praise and glory.
Bless God, ice and cold.
Give praise and glory.

Bless God, frost and sleet.
Give praise and glory.
Bless God, night and day.
Give praise and glory.

Bless God, light and darkness.
Give praise and glory.
Bless God, lightning and clouds.
Give praise and glory for ever.

Bless God, earth and sea.
Give praise and glory.
Bless God, mountains and hills.
Give praise and glory.

Bless God, trees and plants.
Give praise and glory.
Bless God, fountains and springs.
Give praise and glory.

Bless God, rivers and seas.
Give praise and glory.
Bless God, fishes and whales.
Give praise and glory.

Bless God, birds of the air.
Give praise and glory.
Bless God, beasts of the earth.
Give praise and glory for ever.

Bless God, children of earth.
Give praise and glory.
Bless God, Israel.
Give praise and glory.

Bless God, priests of God.
Give praise and glory.
Bless God, servants of God.
Give praise and glory.

Bless God, just and faithful souls.
Give praise and glory.
Bless God, holy and humble hearts.
Give praise and glory.
Bless God, Hananiah, Azariah, and Mishael.
Give praise and glory for ever.

Bless God beyond the stars.
Give praise and glory.
Bless God, heaven and earth.
Give praise and glory for ever. □

PSALM 148

Across the heavens, from the heights,
sing praise, sing praise!

Praise the Lord!
Across the heavens,
from the heights,
all you angels, heavenly beings,
sing praise, sing praise!

Sun and moon, glittering stars,
sing praise, sing praise.
Highest heavens, rain clouds,
sing praise, sing praise.

Praise God's name,
whose word called you forth
and fixed you in place for ever
by eternal decree.

Let there be praise:
from depths of the earth,
from creatures of the deep.

Fire and hail, snow and mist,
storms, winds,
mountains, hills,
fruit trees and cedars,
wild beasts and tame,
snakes and birds,

princes, judges,
rulers, subjects,
men, women,
old and young,
praise, praise the holy name,
this name beyond all names.

God's splendor above the earth,
above the heavens,
gives strength to the nation,
glory to the faithful,
a people close to the Lord.
Israel, let there be praise! □

Praise the Lord, the God of Israel,
who shepherds the people and sets them free...

CANTICLE OF
ZECHARIAH

SUNDAY EVENING PRAYER II

The Lord decrees to the king:
Take the throne at my right hand, hallelujah.

The Lord decrees to the king:
"Take the throne at my right hand,
I will make your enemies a footrest.
I will raise your scepter
over Zion and beyond,
over all your enemies.

"Your people stand behind you
on the day you take command.
You are made holy, splendid,
newborn like the dawn,
fresh like the dew."

God's oath is firm:
"You are a priest for ever,
the rightful king by my decree."
The Lord stands at your side
to destroy kings
on the day of wrath.

God executes judgment,
crushes the heads of nations,
and brings carnage worldwide.
The victor drinks
from a wayside stream
and rises refreshed. □

Who can forget God's wonders,
a God, merciful and kind! hallelujah!

With my whole heart
I praise the Lord among the just.
Great are God's works,
a delight to explore.
In splendor, in majesty,
God's justice will stand.

Who can forget God's wonders!
a God, merciful and kind
who nourished the faithful,
upheld the covenant,
and revealed mighty deeds,
giving them the land of pagans.

Faithful, just, and true
are all God's decrees:
each law in its place,
valid for ever.

The Lord redeems the faithful,
decrees a lasting covenant.
Holy and awesome God's name!

Fear of the Lord is wisdom's crown,
wise are those who live by it.
Praise the Lord for ever! □

The Lord God almighty rules, alleluia!

Alleluia! (*or:* Amen. Alleluia!)
Salvation, glory and power to God!
Alleluia, Alleluia!
Right and sure, the judgments of God!
Alleluia, Alleluia!

Alleluia!
Praise our God, you faithful servants!
Alleluia, Alleluia!
In awe praise God, you small and great!
Alleluia, Alleluia!

Alleluia!
The Lord God almighty rules!
Alleluia, Alleluia!
Be glad, rejoice, give glory to God!
Alleluia, Alleluia!

Alleluia!
The wedding feast of the Lamb begins.
Alleluia, Alleluia!
The bride is radiant, clothed in glory.
Alleluia, Alleluia! (*or:* Amen. Alleluia!) □

Ours were the sufferings Christ bore;
ours the torments he endured.

1 PETER 2:
21 – 24

In Lent

Christ suffered for us
leaving us an example,
that we might walk
in his footsteps.

He did nothing wrong;
no false word
ever passed his lips.

When they cursed him
he returned no curse.
Tortured, he made no threats
but trusted in the perfect judge.

He carried our sins
in his body
to the cross,
that we might die to sin
and live for justice.
When he was wounded,
we were healed. □

I acclaim the greatness of the Lord,
I delight in God my savior...

CANTICLE
OF MARY

PSALM 84

To live with you is joy,
Lord of heaven's might.

Your temple is my joy,
Lord of heaven's might.
I am eager for it,
eager for the courts of God.
My flesh, my flesh sings
its joy to the living God.

As a sparrow homing,
a swallow seeking a nest
to hatch its young,
I am eager for your altars,
Lord of heaven's might,
my king, my God.

To live with you is joy,
to praise you and never stop.
Those you bless with courage
will bless you from their hearts.

When they cross the Valley of Thirst
the ground is spaced with springs,
with the welcome rain of autumn.
They travel the towns to reach
the God of gods in Zion.

Hear me, Lord of might,
heed me, God of Jacob.
God our shield, look,
see the face of your anointed.

One day within your courts
is worth a thousand without.
I would rather stand at God's gate
than move among the wicked.

God is our sun, our shield,
the giver of honor and grace.
The Lord never fails to bless
those who walk with integrity.
Lord of heaven's might,
blest are all who trust in you. □

Let us climb the holy mountain
to the house of Jacob's God.

ISAIAH 2:2 – 5

In the final days
the temple summit will tower
above the highest hills and mountains.
All nations will stream toward it.

Strangers will come and say:
"Let us climb the Lord's mountain
to the house of Jacob's God,
who will teach us the way of truth
and the path we should walk."
From Zion comes instruction,
from Jerusalem, God's word.

God will end conflict between nations,
and settle disputes between peoples;
they will hammer swords to plows,
and spears to pruning knives.

Nations will not take up arms,
will no longer train for war.
House of Jacob, come,
let us walk in the light of the Lord. □

PSALM 96

Sing and bless God's name,
tell God's triumph day to day.

A new song for the Lord!
Sing it and bless God's name,
everyone, everywhere!
Tell the whole world
God's triumph day to day,
God's glory, God's wonder.

A noble God deserving praise,
the dread of other gods,
the puny gods of pagans;
for our God made the heavens —
the Lord of majestic light
who fills the temple with beauty.

Proclaim the Lord, you nations,
praise the glory of God's power,
praise the glory of God's name!
Bring gifts to the temple,
bow down, all the earth,
tremble in God's holy presence.

Tell the nations, "The Lord rules!"
As the firm earth is not swayed,
nothing can sway God's judgment.
Let heaven and earth be glad,
the sea and sea creatures roar,
the field and its beasts exult.

Then let the trees of the forest sing
before the coming of the Lord,
who comes to judge the nations,
to set the earth aright,
restoring the world to order. □

Praise the Lord, the God of Israel,
who shepherds the people and sets them free...

CANTICLE OF
ZECHARIAH

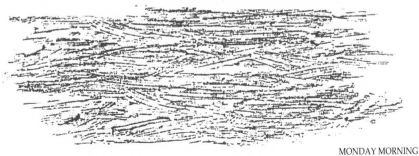

PSALM 123

Our eyes rest on you, Lord,
awaiting your kindness.

I gaze at the heavens,
searching for you, my God.

A slave watches his master's hand,
a servant girl, the hand of her mistress;
so our eyes rest on you, Lord,
awaiting your kindness.

Have mercy, Lord, have mercy.
We have swallowed enough scorn,
stomached enough sneers:
the scoffing of the complacent,
the mockery of the proud. □

PSALM 124

Our help is the Lord,
creator of earth and sky.

Say it, Israel!
If the Lord had not been with us,
if the Lord had not been for us
when enemies rose against us,
they would have swallowed us
in their blazing anger,
and the raging waters
would have swept us away —
rushing, surging water,
thundering over us.

Blessed be the Lord
for saving our flesh from their teeth,
for tearing the trapper's net,
so we could flutter away like birds.
Our help is the Lord,
creator of earth and sky. □

God determined out of love
to adopt us through Jesus Christ.

EPHESIANS 1:
3 – 10

Bless God, the Father of our Lord Jesus Christ,
who blessed us from heaven through Christ
with every blessing of the Spirit.

Before laying the world's foundation,
God chose us in Christ
to live a pure and holy life.

God determined out of love
to adopt us through Jesus Christ
for the praise and glory of that grace
granted us in the Beloved.

By Christ's blood we were redeemed,
our sins forgiven
through extravagant love.

With perfect wisdom and insight
God freely displayed the mystery
of what was always intended:
a plan for the fullness of time
to unite the entire universe through Christ. □

I acclaim the greatness of the Lord,
I delight in God my savior...

TUESDAY MORNING PRAYER

Justice clears God's path,
justice points the way.

Lord, you loved your land,
brought Jacob back,
forgot our guilt,
forgave our sins,
swallowed your anger,
your blazing anger.

Bring us back,
saving God.
End your wrath.
Will it stop,
or drag on for ever?

Turn, revive us,
nourish our joy.
Show us mercy,
save us, Lord!

I listen to God speaking:
"I, the Lord, speak peace,
peace to my faithful people
who turn their hearts to me."
Salvation is coming near,
glory is filling our land.

Love and fidelity embrace,
peace and justice kiss.
Fidelity sprouts from the earth,
justice leans down from heaven.

The Lord pours out riches,
our land springs to life.
Justice clears God's path,
justice points the way. □

ISAIAH 26:
1 – 4, 7 – 9, 12

I long for you by night,
my whole being yearns for you.

Our city is strong,
its ramparts and walls
are God's saving work.
Throw open the gates
to a just nation,
one that keeps faith.

You guard the faithful in peace,
they fix their hearts on you.
Trust in the Lord always,
our enduring rock.

For the just you make the road
level, smooth, and straight.
We walk the road you cut,
looking for you, O Lord.
We seek to honor your name.

I long for you by night,
my whole being yearns for you.
For by your judgments
the world learns justice.
Our peace is your gift, Lord,
our good deeds your work. □

Lord, let your face shine on us,
revealing your way to all peoples.

PSALM 67

Favor and bless us, Lord.
Let your face shine on us,
revealing your way to all peoples,
salvation the world over.

Let nations sing your praise,
every nation on earth.

The world will shout for joy,
for you rule the planet with justice.
In fairness you govern the nations
and guide the peoples of earth.

Let the nations sing your praise,
every nation on earth.

The land delivers its harvest,
God, our God, has blessed us.
O God, continue your blessing,
may the whole world worship you. □

Praise the Lord, the God of Israel,
who shepherds the people and sets them free…

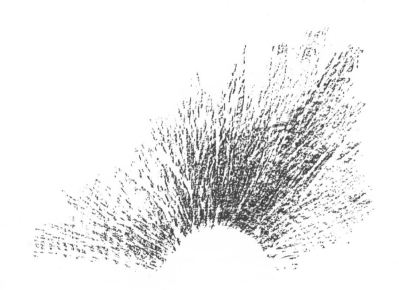

TUESDAY EVENING PRAYER

As mountains circle Jerusalem,
Lord, you embrace your people.

Those who trust the Lord
stand firm as Zion,
solid and strong.

As mountains circle Jerusalem,
Lord, you embrace your people
now and for ever.

Keep the rule of the wicked
far from the land of the just,
or the just may turn to evil.

Lord, show your goodness
to those who do good,
whose hearts are true.

Away with the devious,
banish them with the wicked!
Give Israel peace! □

PSALM 131   *My whole being is at rest in you, my God.*

Lord, I am not proud,
holding my head too high,
reaching beyond my grasp.

No, I am calm and tranquil
like a weaned child
resting in its mother's arms:
my whole being at rest.

Let Israel rest in the Lord,
now and for ever. □

REVELATION   *Christ Jesus, your blood purchased for God*
4:11; 5:9 – 10, 12   *every tribe, language, people and nation.*

Worthy are you, Lord God,
to receive glory, honor and power,
for you are creator and source of all.

Worthy are you, O Christ,
to take the scroll and break the seals,
for you were slain,
and your blood purchased for God
every tribe, language, people and nation.

You made them royal priests
to serve our God,
and they will rule on earth.

Worthy is the slaughtered Lamb,
worthy of power and wealth,
wisdom and strength,
honor and glory and praise. □

I acclaim the greatness of the Lord,
I delight in God my savior...

CANTICLE
OF MARY

PSALM 86

Bring joy to me, your servant, Lord,
I offer myself to you.

Hear me, Lord, and act,
I am poor and helpless.
You are my God,
watch over me,
for I am loyal to you.
Save me, your servant,
for I trust you.

Each waking hour
I beg your mercy, Lord.
Bring joy to me, your servant,
I offer myself to you.
You are good and forgiving,
loyal to all who call on you.

Hear my prayer, O Lord,
answer my cry for help.
In my despair I plead,
knowing you will act.
No god can match you, Lord,
you outdo all others.

Every nation you formed
will come to worship
and honor your name.
You are mighty
and work great wonders.
You alone are God!

Mark your path, Lord,
that I may follow your truth.
Make my one desire
to revere your name.

With all I am, I thank you, God,
and honor your name for ever.
Your love for me is great,
it saves me from the grave.

The proud rise against me,
brutal gangs seek my life,
with no thought of you.
But you are Lord of mercy and care,
a God slow to anger,
full of loyalty and love.

Turn to me, pity me,
strengthen your daughter's child,
rescue your servant.
Show me a sign of your love
to shock and disgrace my enemy.
Bring help and comfort, Lord. □

Only the honest in word and deed
are safe with God.

ISAIAH 33:
13 – 16

Listen, my people,
far-off and nearby.
See what I do,
know my power.

Terror grips the wicked in Zion;
the godless shake with fear.
Who can face the fiery judgment?
Who can endure the lasting flames?

Only the honest in word and deed
who refuse to exploit others,
who turn down bribes,
who will not hear of bloodshed
or dare to imagine crimes.

They live secure and safe
as in a mountain fort
with plenty to eat and drink. □

PSALM 98

With sound of trumpet and horn,
shout to the Lord, our king.

Sing to the Lord a new song,
the Lord of wonderful deeds.
Right hand and holy arm
brought victory to God.

God made that victory known,
revealed justice to nations,
remembered a merciful love
loyal to the house of Israel.
The ends of the earth have seen
the victory of our God.

Shout to the Lord, you earth,
break into song, into praise!
Sing praise to God with a harp,
with a harp and sound of music.
With sound of trumpet and horn,
shout to the Lord, our king.

Let the sea roar with its creatures,
the world and all that live there!
Let rivers clap their hands,
the hills ring out their joy!

The Lord our God comes,
comes to rule the earth,
justly to rule the world,
to govern the peoples aright. □

Praise the Lord, the God of Israel,
who shepherds the people and sets them free...

CANTICLE OF
ZECHARIAH

WEDNESDAY EVENING PRAYER

PSALM 126

Those sowing in tears
reap, singing and laughing.

The Lord brings us back to Zion,
we are like dreamers,
laughing, dancing,
with songs on our lips.

Other nations say,
"A new world of wonders!
The Lord is with them."
Yes, God works wonders.
Rejoice! Be glad!

Lord, bring us back
as water to thirsty land.
Those sowing in tears
reap, singing and laughing.

They left weeping, weeping,
casting the seed.
They come back singing, singing,
holding high the harvest. □

PSALM 127

May God build our house
and watch over our city.

If God does not build the house,
the builders work in vain.
If God does not watch over the city,
the guards watch in vain.

How foolish to rise early
and slave until night for bread.
Those who please God receive as much
even while they sleep.

Children are God's gift,
a blessing to those who bear them;
like arrows in the hand of an archer
are children born to the young.
Happy those with a full quiver:
facing their enemies at the gate,
they stand without shame! □

*Christi is firstborn in all creation
and in all things first.*

COLOSSIANS
1:12 – 20

Give thanks to the Father,
who made us fit
for the holy community of light
and rescued us from darkness,
bringing us into the realm
of his beloved Son
who redeemed us,
forgiving our sins.

Christ is an image
of the God we cannot see.
Christ is firstborn in all creation.

Through Christ the universe was made,
things seen and unseen,
thrones, authorities, forces, powers.
Everything was created
through Christ and for Christ.

Before anything came to be, Christ was,
and the universe is held together by Christ.

Christ is also head of the body, the church,
its beginning as firstborn from the dead
to become in all things first.

For by God's good pleasure
Christ encompasses
the full measure of power,
reconciling creation with its source
and making peace by the blood of the cross. ☐

CANTICLE
OF MARY

I acclaim the greatness of the Lord,
I delight in God my savior…

THURSDAY MORNING PRAYER

Great is your renown, city of God.

PSALM 87

Zion is set on the holy mountain.
The Lord loves her gates
above all the dwellings of Israel.
Great is your renown, city of God.

I register as her citizens
Egypt and Babylon,
Philistia, Ethiopia, and Tyre:
"Each one was born in her."

People will say, "Zion mothered
each and every one."
The Most High protects the city.

God records in the register,
"This one was born here."
Then people will dance and sing,
"My home is here!" □

Look, the Lord comes;
see what spoils the victor brings!

ISAIAH 40:
10 – 17

Look! the Lord comes.
What power God holds!
See what spoils the victor brings!

As the shepherd tends the flock,
the Lord gathers the lambs
in a warm embrace
and leads the nursing sheep.

Who can scoop up the oceans
or span the heavens with one hand?
Who can hold the earth in a measure,
weigh the mountains on scales,
the hills on a balance?

Who directed the Lord's spirit?
What mortal counseled God?
Whose advice did God seek?
Whose teaching on the way of justice?
Whose guidance on the path to wisdom?

The nations are like a drop of water,
a speck of dust on the scales.
The Lord lifts up islands like sand.

Lebanon has neither wood enough
nor beasts enough for sacrifice.
In God's sight the nations are nothing.
They are empty as a void. □

PSALM 99

Bow down to worship God,
give praise in this holy place.

The Lord reigns from the cherubim throne,
nations tremble, earth shakes!
The Lord of Zion is great,
high above all peoples.
Praise the great and fearful name,
"Holy is the Lord!"

Almighty ruler, you love justice,
you strengthen the upright
and secure equity for Jacob.
Bow down to worship at God's feet,
lift your voice in praise,
"Holy is the Lord!"

First among priests of the Lord
were Moses, Aaron, and Samuel;
they called out God's Name.
The Lord heard them
and spoke from a pillar of cloud;
they honored each command.

Our God did what was needed,
it was yours, Lord, to punish,
yours to forgive sin.
Bow down to worship the Lord,
give praise in God's holy place,
"Holy is the Lord our God!" □

Praise the Lord, the God of Israel,
who shepherds the people and sets them free...

CANTICLE OF
ZECHARIAH

THURSDAY EVENING PRAYER

Lord, let your saints rejoice
as they go to your house.

Lord, remember David
in all his humility.
He swore an oath to you,
O Mighty God of Jacob:

"I will not enter my home,
nor lie down on my bed.
I will not close my eyes
nor will I sleep
until I find a place for the Lord,
a house for the Mighty God of Jacob."

We heard about it in Ephrata,
in the fields of Yaarim:
"Let us go to God's house,
let us worship at God's throne."

Lord, come to your resting place,
you and your ark of power.
May your priests dress for the feast,
and your faithful shout for joy. □

I will bless Zion with abundance,
even the poor will have food.

Be loyal to David, your servant,
do not reject your anointed.
You once swore to David
and will not break your word:
"Your child will ascend your throne.

"If your heirs then keep my laws,
if they keep my covenant,
their children will rule
from your throne for ever."

The Lord has chosen Zion,
desired it as a home.
"This is my resting place,
I choose to live here for ever.

"I will bless it with abundance,
even the poor will have food.
I will vest the priests in holiness,
and the faithful will shout for joy.

"Here I will strengthen David's power
and light a lamp for my anointed.
His enemies I will clothe in shame,
but on him a crown will shine." □

God has given Christ all glory, honor and praise;
every nation shall serve him.

We thank you, Lord,
God and ruler of all,
who is and who was.
You have claimed your power
and begun to reign.

When the nations raged
your anger stirred.
Then was the moment
to judge the dead,
to reward your servants, the prophets,
to honor your holy ones
who honored your name,
small and great alike.

Now is salvation,
the power and reign of God;
the Christ holds command.
For the one who accused the saints
day and night before God
has now been driven out.

They won the battle
by the blood of the Lamb,
and by the power of their witness
despite the threat of death.
Citizens of heaven, rejoice. □

I acclaim the greatness of the Lord,
I delight in God my savior…

CANTICLE
OF MARY

FRIDAY MORNING PRAYER

Have mercy, tender God,
forget that I defied you.

Have mercy, tender God,
forget that I defied you.
Wash away my sin,
cleanse me from my guilt.

I know my evil well,
it stares me in the face,
evil done to you alone
before your very eyes.

How right your condemnation!
Your verdict clearly just.
You see me for what I am,
a sinner before my birth.

You love those centered in truth;
teach me your hidden wisdom.
Wash me with fresh water,
wash me bright as snow.

Fill me with happy songs,
let the bones you bruised now dance.
Shut your eyes to my sin,
make my guilt disappear.

Creator, reshape my heart,
God, steady my spirit.
Do not cast me aside
stripped of your holy spirit.

Save me, bring back my joy,
support me, strengthen my will.
Then I will teach your way
and sinners will turn to you.

Help me, stop my tears,
and I will sing your goodness.
Lord, give me words
and I will shout your praise.

When I offer a holocaust,
the gift does not please you.
So I offer my shattered spirit;
a changed heart you welcome.

In your love make Zion lovely,
rebuild the walls of Jerusalem.
Then sacrifice will please you,
young bulls upon your altar. □

God, we have sinned against you,
we share our people's guilt.

JEREMIAH 14:
17 – 21

Day and night
my tears never stop,
for my people are struck,
my daughter crushed
by a savage blow.

I see the dead slain in the fields
and people starving on city streets.
Priest and prophet wander about,
not knowing where to turn.

Lord, have you nothing
but contempt for Zion?
Have you completely rejected Judah?
Why have you inflicted wounds
that do not heal?

We long for peace,
we long for healing,
but there is only terror.
We have sinned against you
and we know it, God;
we share our people's guilt.

For the sake of your name,
do not abandon us.
For the honor of your throne,
remember your covenant,
do not break your oath. □

The Lord is our shepherd and we the flock.   PSALM 100

Shout joy to the <u>Lord</u>, all earth,
serve the <u>Lord</u> with gladness,
enter God's pres<u>ence</u> with joy!

Know that the <u>Lord</u> is God,
our maker to whom <u>we</u> belong,
our shepherd, and <u>we</u> the flock.

Enter the <u>tem</u>ple gates,
the courtyard with <u>thanks</u> and praise;
give thanks and <u>bless</u> God's name.

Indeed the <u>Lord</u> is good!
God's love <u>is</u> for ever,
faithful from <u>age</u> to age. □

Praise the Lord, the <u>God</u> of Israel,   CANTICLE OF
who shepherds the people and <u>sets</u> them free...   ZECHARIAH

FRIDAY EVENING PRAYER

PSALM 135:
1 – 12

Sing hymns, for God is good;
sing God's name, our delight.

Praise the name of the Lord,
give praise, faithful servants,
who stand in the courtyard,
gathered at God's house.

Sing hymns, for God is good.
Sing God's name, our delight,
for the Lord chose Jacob,
Israel as a special treasure.

I know the Lord is great,
surpassing every little god.
What God wills, God does
in heaven and earth,
in the deepest sea.

God blankets earth with clouds,
strikes lightning for the rain,
releases wind from the storehouse.

God killed Egypt's firstborn,
both humans and beasts,
doing wondrous signs in Egypt
against Pharoah and his aides.

God struck down nations,
killed mighty kings,
Sihon, king of the Amorites,
Og, king of Bashan,
all the kings of Canaan.

Then God gave Israel their land,
a gift for them to keep. □

Bless God, house of Israel;
sing God's name, our delight.

Your name lives for ever, Lord,
your renown never fades,
for you give your people justice
and attend to their needs.

Pagan idols are silver and gold
crafted by human hands.
Their mouths cannot speak,
their eyes do not see.

Their ears hear nothing,
their nostrils do not breathe.
Their makers who rely on them
become like these hollow images.

Bless God, house of Israel,
house of Aaron, house of Levi,
every faithful one.

Blest be the Lord of Zion,
who calls Jerusalem home.

Hallelujah! □

All nations will gather,
bowing low to you, O God.

All you do stirs wonder,
Lord, mighty God.
Your ways are right and true,
ruler of all nations.

Who would not be moved
to glorify your name?
For you alone are holy.

All nations will gather,
bowing low to you,
for your saving works
are plainly seen. □

I acclaim the greatness of the Lord,
I delight in God my savior...

SATURDAY MORNING PRAYER

You, O Lord, are close;
your law is my whole truth.

PSALM 119:
145 – 152

My heart begs you, Lord:
hear me, so I can keep faith.
I beg you, make me free,
so I can live your laws.

I face you in the cold night
praying, waiting for your word.
I keep watch through the night,
repeating what you promise.

Hear me, loving God,
let your justice make me live.
The wicked close in on me;
to them your law is foreign.

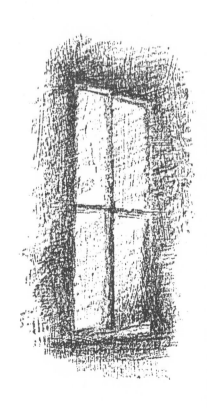

But you, Lord, are closer still,
your law is my whole truth,
learned when I was young,
fixed for all time. □

Send Wisdom from heaven to be my companion,
to teach me your will.

Merciful God of my ancestors,
with a word you created all things;
in wisdom you made humankind
to care for your creatures
with holiness and justice,
to rule with upright heart.

Give me Wisdom who sits by your throne;
never forget I am your child,
your servant born of your handmaid,
frail, given little time,
with limited grasp of your laws.
Yet even someone perfect
is nothing without the Wisdom
that comes from you.

With you is Wisdom;
she knows your works,
was there when you made the world.
She sees what you judge as best,
knows what is right in your commands.

Send her from heaven,
from your glorious throne
to be my companion,
to teach me your will.

Her understanding is complete;
she guides me wisely
through all I must do,
and guards me with her clear light. □

Strong the love embracing us.
Faithful the Lord for ever.

PSALM 117

Praise! Give glory to God!
Nations, peoples, give glory!

Strong the love embracing us.
Faithful the Lord for ever.

Hallelujah! □

Praise the Lord, the God of Israel,
who shepherds the people and sets them free...

CANTICLE OF
ZECHARIAH

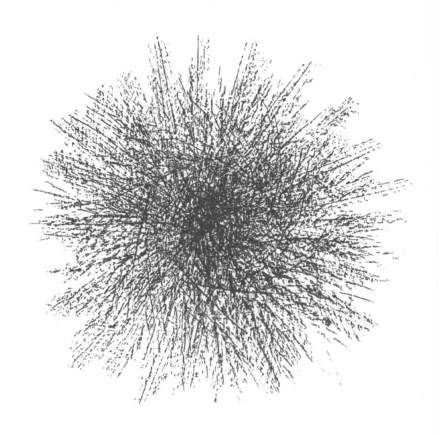

SUNDAY
Week IV

SUNDAY EVENING PRAYER I

With joy I heard them say,
"Let us go to the Lord's house."

With joy I <u>heard</u> them say,
"Let us go to the <u>Lord's</u> house!"
And <u>now</u>, Jerusalem,
we stand in<u>side</u> your gates.

Jerusalem, the cit<u>y</u> so built
that city and temp<u>le</u> are one.
To you the <u>tribes</u> go up,
every tribe <u>of</u> the Lord.

It is the <u>law</u> of Israel
to hon<u>or</u> God's name.
The seats of <u>law</u> are here,
the thrones of <u>Da</u>vid's line.

Pray peace <u>for</u> Jerusalem:
happiness <u>for</u> your homes,
safety in<u>side</u> your walls,
peace in <u>your</u> great houses.

For love of fami<u>ly</u> and friends
I say, "Peace <u>be</u> with you!"
For love of the <u>Lord's</u> own house
I pray <u>for</u> your good. □

From morning watch until night,
I waited for the Lord.

From the depths I call to you,
Lord, hear my cry.
Catch the sound of my voice
raised up, pleading.

If you record our sins,
Lord, who could survive?
But because you forgive
we stand in awe.

I trust in God's word,
I trust in the Lord.
More than sentries for dawn
I watch for the Lord.

More than sentries for dawn
let Israel watch.
The Lord will bring mercy
and grant full pardon.
The Lord will free Israel
from all its sins. □

*At the name of Jesus every knee will bend
in heaven and on earth.*

Though in the form of God,
Jesus did not claim
equality with God
but emptied himself,
taking the form of a slave,
human like one of us.

Flesh and blood,
he humbled himself,
obeying to the death,
death on a cross.
For this very reason
God lifted him high
and gave him the name
above all names.

So at the name of Jesus
every knee will bend
in heaven, on earth,
and in the world below,
and every tongue exclaim
to the glory of God the Father,
"Jesus Christ is Lord." □

I acclaim the greatness of the Lord,
I delight in God my savior...

SUNDAY MORNING PRAYER

This is the day the Lord has made,
let us rejoice and be glad.

Give thanks, the Lord is good,
God's love is for ever!
Now let Israel say,
"God's love is for ever!"

Let the house of Aaron say,
"God's love is for ever!"
Let all who revere the Lord say,
"God's love is for ever!"

In distress I called to the Lord,
who answered and set me free.
The Lord is with me, I fear not.
What can they do to me?
The Lord my help is with me,
I can face my foes.

Better to trust in the Lord
than rely on human help.
Better to trust in the Lord
than rely on generous hearts.

The nations surrounded me;
in God's name, I will crush them!
Surrounded me completely;
in God's name, I will crush them!
Surrounded me like bees,
blazed like brushwood fire;
in God's name, I will crush them!

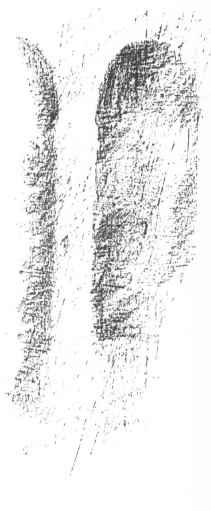

I was pushed to falling,
but the Lord gave me help.
My strength, my song is the Lord,
who has become my savior.

Glad songs of victory sound
within the tents of the just.
With right hand raised high,
the Lord strikes with force.

I shall not die but live
to tell the Lord's great deeds.
The Lord punished me severely,
but did not let me die.

Open the gates of justice,
let me praise God within them.
This is the Lord's own gate,
only the just will enter.
I thank you for you answered me,
and you became my savior.

The stone the builders rejected
has become the cornerstone.
This is the work of the Lord,
how wonderful in our eyes.

This is the day the Lord made,
let us rejoice and be glad.
Lord, give us the victory!
Lord, grant us success!

Blest is the one who comes,
who comes in the name of the Lord.
We bless you from the Lord's house.
The Lord God is our light:
adorn the altar with branches.

I will thank you, my God,
I will praise you highly.
Give thanks, the Lord is good,
God's love is for ever! ☐

Sing a hymn of praise to our God, hallelujah!

DANIEL 3:
52 – 57

Blest are you, God of our ancestors,
praised and lifted above all for ever!
Blest your holy name, full of wonder,
praised and lifted above all for ever!

Blest are you in your temple of glory,
acclaimed and honored for ever.
Blest are you who see the depths
from the cherubim throne,
praised and lifted above all for ever!

Blest are you enthroned in majesty,
praised and lifted above all for ever!
Blest are you beyond the stars,
acclaimed and honored for ever!

All you creatures, bless our God,
acclaimed and exalted for ever! ☐

All that is alive, praise.
Praise God. Hallelujah!

Praise! Praise God in the temple,
in the highest heavens!
Praise! Praise God's mighty deeds
and noble majesty.

Praise! Praise God with trumpet blasts,
with lute and harp.
Praise! Praise God with timbrel and dance,
with strings and pipes.

Praise! Praise God with crashing cymbals,
with ringing cymbals.
All that is alive, praise. Praise the Lord.
Hallelujah! □

CANTICLE OF
ZECHARIAH

Praise the Lord, the God of Israel,
who sheperds the people and sets them free...

SUNDAY EVENING PRAYER II

You are newborn like the dawn,
fresh like the dew.

PSALM 110

The Lord decrees to the king:
"Take the throne at my right hand,
I will make your enemies a footrest.
I will raise your scepter
over Zion and beyond,
over all your enemies.

"Your people stand behind you
on the day you take command.
You are made holy, splendid,
newborn like the dawn,
fresh like the dew."

God's oath is firm:
"You are a priest for ever,
the rightful king by my decree."
The Lord stands at your side
to destroy kings
on the day of wrath.

God executes judgment,
crushes the heads of nations,
and brings carnage worldwide.
The victor drinks
from a wayside stream
and rises refreshed. □

PSALM 112

Happy are those who love God,
a God of mercy and justice.

Happy those who love God
and delight in the law.
Their children shall be blest,
strong and upright in the land.

Their households thrive,
their integrity stands firm.
A light shines on them in darkness,
a God of mercy and justice.

The good lend freely
and deal fairly,
they will never stumble;
their justice shall be remembered.

Bad news holds no power,
strong hearts trust God.
Steady and fearless,
they look down on their enemy.

They support the poor,
their integrity stands firm,
their strength brings them honor.

Hatred devours the wicked.
They grind their teeth;
their hopes turn to ashes. □

Praise our God, you faithful servants!
In awe praise God, alleluia.

Alleluia! (*or:* Amen. Alleluia!)
Salvation, glory and power to God!
Alleluia, Alleluia!
Right and sure, the judgments of God!
Alleluia, Alleluia!

Alleluia!
Praise our God, you faithful servants!
Alleluia, Alleluia!
In awe praise God, you small and great!
Alleluia, Alleluia!

Alleluia!
The Lord God almighty rules!
Alleluia, Alleluia!
Be glad, rejoice, give glory to God!
Alleluia, Alleluia!

Alleluia!
The wedding feast of the Lamb begins.
Alleluia, Alleluia!
The bride is radiant, clothed in glory.
Alleluia, Alleluia! (*or:* Amen. Alleluia!) □

1 PETER 2:
21 – 24

In Lent

*These things foretold by God through the prophets
concerning Christ's suffering
are now fulfilled.*

Christ suffered for us
leaving us an example,
that we might walk
in his footsteps.

He did nothing wrong;
no false word
ever passed his lips.

When they cursed him
he returned no curse.
Tortured, he made no threats
but trusted in the perfect judge.

He carried our sins
in his body
to the cross,
that we might die to sin
and live for justice.
When he was wounded,
we were healed. □

CANTICLE
OF MARY

I acclaim the greatness of the Lord,
I delight in God my savior…

MONDAY MORNING PRAYER

Shine your love on us each dawn
and gladden all our days.

You have been our haven, Lord,
from generation to generation.
Before the mountains existed,
before the earth was born,
from age to age you are God.

You return us to dust,
children of earth back to earth.
For in your eyes a thousand years
are like a single day:
they pass with the swiftness of sleep.

You sweep away the years
as sleep passes at dawn,
like grass that springs up in the day
and is withered by evening.

For we perish at your wrath,
your anger strikes terror.
You lay bare our sins
in the piercing light of your presence.
All our days wither beneath your glance,
our lives vanish like a breath.

Our life is a mere seventy years,
eighty with good health,
and all it gives us
is toil and distress;
then the thread breaks
and we are gone.

Who can know the force of your anger?
Your fury matches our fear.
Teach us to make use of our days
and bring wisdom to our hearts.

How long, O Lord, before you return?
Pity your servants,
shine your love on us each dawn,
and gladden all our days.

Balance our past sorrows
with present joys
and let your servants, young and old,
see the splendor of your work.
Let your loveliness shine on us,
and bless the work we do,
bless the work of our hands. □

ISAIAH 42:
10 – 16

Let the coastland and its people
fill the world with praise.

Sing the Lord a new song.
Let the sea with its creatures,
the coastland and its people
fill the world with praise.

Let every village and town,
from Kedar on the plain
to Sela in the hills,
take up the joyful song.
Sing glory to the Lord,
give praise across the world.

The Lord strides like a hero
who rouses fury
with a great battle cry
and charges against the enemy.

"I have kept quiet too long,
too long held back.
Like a woman in labor
I now scream and cry out:

"I will lay waste mountains and hills
and stunt all their greenery.
I will dry up rivers and pools
and create an arid wasteland.

"I will lead the blind safely
along strange roads.
I will make their darkness light,
their winding ways straight.
I will do all this,
I will not fail them." □

Praise the name of the Lord,
you faithful servants gathered at God's house.

Praise the name of the Lord,
give praise, faithful servants,
who stand in the courtyard,
gathered at God's house.

Sing hymns, for God is good.
Sing God's name, our delight,
for the Lord chose Jacob,
Israel as a special treasure.

I know the Lord is great,
surpassing every little god.
What God wills, God does
in heaven and earth,
in the deepest sea.

God blankets earth with clouds,
strikes lightning for the rain,
releases wind from the storehouse.

God killed Egypt's firstborn,
both humans and beasts,
doing wondrous signs in Egypt
against Pharoah and his aides.

God struck down nations,
killed mighty kings,
Sihon, king of the Amorites,
Og, king of Bashan,
all the kings of Canaan.

Then God gave Israel their land,
a gift for them to keep. □

Praise the Lord, the God of Israel,
who shepherds the people and sets them free...

CANTICLE OF
ZECHARIAH

MONDAY EVENING PRAYER

PSALM 136:
1 – 9

*Where charity and love are found,
there is God.*

Our God is good, give thanks!
God's love is for ever!
Our God of gods, give thanks!
God's love is for ever!
Our Lord of lords, give thanks!
God's love is for ever!

Alone the maker of worlds!
God's love is for ever!
Architect for the skies!
God's love is for ever!
Spread land on the sea!
God's love is for ever!

Set the great lights above!
God's love is for ever!
The sun to rule the day!
God's love is for ever!
The moon and stars, the night!
God's love is for ever! □

Great and wonderful are your deeds,
Lord God almighty.

Struck down Egypt's firstborn!
God's love is for ever!
Guided Israel's escape!
God's love is for ever!
Held out a mighty arm!
God's love is for ever!

Split in two the Reed Sea!
God's love is for ever!
Led Israel across!
God's love is for ever!
Drowned Pharaoh and his troops!
God's love is for ever!

Led the desert trek!
God's love is for ever!
Struck down mighty tribes!
God's love is for ever!
Killed powerful kings!
God's love is for ever!

Sihon, the Amorite king!
God's love is for ever!
And Og, Bashan's king!
God's love is for ever!
Gave Israel a land!
God's love is for ever!
For God's servant to keep!
God's love is for ever!

Remembered our distress!
God's love is for ever!
Kept us from defeat!
God's love is for ever!
God feeds all living things!
God's love is for ever!
God in heaven, be thanked!
God's love is for ever! □

EPHESIANS 1:
3 – 10

In the fullness of time
God planned to unite the entire universe
through Christ.

Bless God, the Father of our Lord Jesus Christ,
who blessed us from heaven through Christ
with every blessing of the Spirit.

Before laying the world's foundation,
God chose us in Christ
to live a pure and holy life.

God determined out of love
to adopt us through Jesus Christ
for the praise and glory of that grace
granted us in the Beloved.

By Christ's blood we were redeemed,
our sins forgiven
through extravagant love.

With perfect wisdom and insight
God freely displayed the mystery
of what was always intended:
a plan for the fullness of time
to unite the entire universe through Christ. □

I acclaim the greatness of the Lord,
I delight in God my savior...

CANTICLE
OF MARY

TUESDAY MORNING PRAYER

PSALM 101

I sing to you, my God,
and live the truth I sing.

I sing to you, O Lord,
sing your justice and love,
and live the truth I sing.
When will you come to me?

I show my royal household
how to lead a perfect life.
I shun what is devious
and hate deceit —
it can never touch me.

The wicked dare not approach me,
for I am no friend to evil.
I silence those who gossip,
I detest their vanity and pride.

I look for loyal people
to share my palace.
Those who live honest lives
will serve me.

I cannot bear scoundrels and liars,
they are not welcome in my house.
My daily work
is to rid the land of evil
and cleanse the City of God. □

Do not withhold your love from us, O Lord.

DANIEL 3:26,
27, 29, 34 – 41

Blest are you, Lord,
God of our ancestors,
worthy of praise
and renowned for ever.

Your works are true,
your ways straight,
your judgments sound,
all your actions just.

We broke your law,
we strayed from you,
sinning in every way.

For the sake of your good name,
do not abandon us,
do not break your oath.
Think of your beloved Abraham,
your servant Isaac, your holy Israel,
and do not withhold your love.

You promised them descendants
countless as the stars,
like sand on the shore.
Yet we are the weakest of nations,
disgraced before all by our sins.

We have no king,
no prophet, no leader,
no burnt offering, no sacrifice,
no gift, no incense, no temple,
nowhere to find mercy.

Let a crushed heart and spirit
mean as much as countless offerings
of rams and sheep and bulls.
Let this be our sacrifice today,
let our loyalty win your favor,
for trust in you brings no shame.

Our hearts are completely yours.
We fear yet seek your presence.
Do not shame us. □

PSALM 144

I sing you a new song, Lord,
I play my ten-stringed harp.

Praise God, God my rock
who trains my hands for battle,
my arms for war.

God, my love, my safety,
my stronghold and defender,
God, my shield, my refuge,
you give me victory.

Who are we that you care for us?
Why give a thought to mortals?
We are little more than breath;
our days, fleeting shadows.

Come, Lord, lower the heavens,
touch the mountains,
let them spew out smoke.
Strike lightning,
let your arrows fly,
scatter my enemies in terror.

Reach down from the heavens,
snatch me from crashing waves;
rescue me from strangers
who speak lies
and then swear to them.

I sing you a new song, Lord,
I play my ten-stringed harp,
for you give victory to kings,
you rescue your servant, David.

Save me from the bitter sword,
deliver me from strangers,
who speak lies
and then swear to them.

God, you shape our sons
like tall, sturdy plants;
you sculpt our daughters
like pillars for a palace.

You fill our barns
with all kinds of food,
you bless our fields
with sheep by the thousands
and fatten all our cattle.

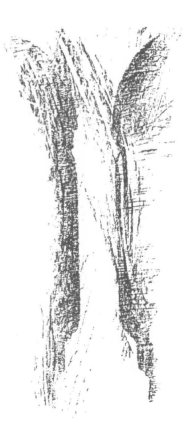

There is no breach in the walls,
no outcry in the streets, no exile.
We are a people blest with these gifts,
blest with the Lord as our God! □

<table>
<tr><td>

CANTICLE OF
ZECHARIAH
</td><td>

Praise the Lord, the God of Israel,
who shepherds the people and sets them free…
</td></tr>
</table>

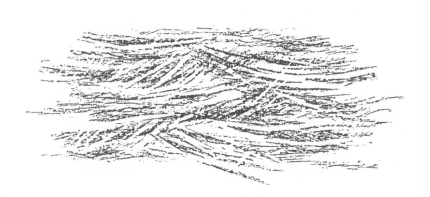

TUESDAY EVENING PRAYER

By the rivers of Babylon we sat weeping;
on the poplars we hung up our harps.

PSALM 137

By the rivers of Babylon
we sat weeping,
remembering Zion.
There on the poplars
we hung our harps.

Our captors shouted
for happy songs,
for songs of festival.
"Sing!" they cried,
"the songs of Zion."

How could we sing
the song of the Lord
in a foreign land?

Jerusalem forgotten?
Wither my hand!
Jerusalem forgotten?
Silence my voice!
if I do not seek you
as my greatest joy.

Lord, never forget
that crime of Edom
against your city,
the day they cried,
"Strip! Smash her to the ground!"

Doomed Babylon, be cursed!
Good for those who deal you
evil for evil!
Good for those who destroy you,
who smash your children at the walls. □

I join heaven's chorus,
praising your love and fidelity.

I thank you with all I am,
I join heaven's chorus.
I bow toward your holy temple,
to praise your name.

By your love and fidelity,
you display to all
the glory of your name and promise.
As soon as I call, you act,
renewing my strength.

Around the world,
rulers praise you
for your commanding word.
They sing of your ways,
"Great is your glory, Lord."

Though high up,
you see the lowly;
though far away,
you keep an eye on the proud.

When I face an opponent,
you keep me alive.
You reach out your hand,
your right hand saves me.

Lord, take up my cause,
your love lasts for ever.
Do not abandon
what your hands have made. □

Worthy is the slaughtered Lamb,
worthy of honor and glory and praise.

REVELATION
4:11; 5:9 – 10, 12

Worthy are you, Lord God,
to receive glory, honor and power,
for you are creator and source of all.

Worthy are you, O Christ,
to take the scroll and break the seals,
for you were slain,
and your blood purchased for God
every tribe, language, people and nation.

You made them royal priests,
to serve our God,
and they will rule on earth.

Worthy is the slaughtered Lamb,
worthy of power and wealth,
wisdom and strength,
honor and glory and praise. □

<table>
<tr><td>CANTICLE
OF MARY</td><td>I acclaim the greatness of the Lord,
I delight in God my savior…</td></tr>
</table>

WEDNESDAY MORNING PRAYER

God, your love is boundless,
stretching beyond the stars.

I have decided, O God,
I will sing of your glory,
will sing your praise.
Awake, my harp and lyre,
so I can wake up the dawn.

I will lift my voice,
sing of you, Lord, to all nations.
For your love fills the heavens,
your unfailing love, the sky.

O God, rise high above the heavens!
Spread your glory across the earth!
Deliver those you love,
use your strength to rescue me.

God decreed in the temple:
"I give away Shechem,
parcel out Succoth.
Manasseh and Gilead are mine.

"With Ephraim as my helmet,
and Judah my spear,
I will make Moab my wash bowl,
trample Edom under my feet,
and over Philistia shout in triumph."

Who will help me, Lord,
scale the heights of Edom
and breach the city wall?
God, will you keep holding back?
Will you desert our camp?

Stand by us against the enemy,
all other aid is worthless.
With you the battle is ours,
you will crush our foes. □

<table>
<tr><td>ISAIAH 61:
10 — 62:7</td><td>*The Lord, my God, has dressed me
in robes of justice and victory.*</td></tr>
</table>

I sing out with joy to the Lord,
all I am delights in God,
for the Lord has dressed me
in robes of justice and victory,
like a groom wearing a garland
or a bride arrayed in jewels.

As earth causes seed to sprout,
and gardens make plants grow,
so justice and praise spring from God
for all the nations to see.

For Zion's sake I speak out,
for Jerusalem I do not rest,
till her victory shines like the sun,
blazes out like a torch.

The world will see your deliverance,
all kings witness your glory.
They will know you by a new name
which the Lord will give you.
Your walls and towers will shine forth,
a royal crown in God's hand.

They will no longer call you Forsaken,
nor your land Barren.
Beloved will be your name,
and your land will be called Married.
For the Lord delights in you,
and your fields will be fertile.

As a young man marries a wife,
your Builder will marry you.
As a groom delights in his bride,
the Lord will honor you.

"On your walls, Jerusalem,
I have posted guards
to stay alert
both day and night."

Stay awake, you advocates,
and give God no rest
till Jerusalem is built up
to become earth's crown. □

My whole life, give praise to God.

Praise the Lord, my heart!
My whole life, give praise.
Let me sing to God
as long as I live.

Never depend on rulers:
born of earth, they cannot save.
They die, they turn to dust.
That day, their plans crumble.

They are wise who depend on God,
who look to Jacob's Lord,
creator of heaven and earth,
maker of the teeming sea.

The Lord keeps faith for ever,
giving food to the hungry,
justice to the poor,
freedom to captives.

The Lord opens blind eyes
and straightens the bent,
comforting widows and orphans,
protecting the stranger.
The Lord loves the just
but blocks the path of the wicked.

Zion, praise the Lord!
Your God reigns for ever,
from generation to generation.
Hallelujah! ☐

Praise the Lord, the God of Israel,
who shepherds the people and sets them free...

CANTICLE OF
ZECHARIAH

WEDNESDAY EVENING PRAYER

Your wisdom overwhelms me, Lord:
too much to understand!

You search me, Lord, and know me.
Wherever I sit or stand,
you read my inmost thoughts;
whenever I walk or rest,
you know where I have been.

Before a word slips from my tongue,
Lord, you know what I will say.
You close in on me,
pressing your hand upon me.
All this overwhelms me —
too much to understand!

Where can I hide from you?
How can I escape your presence?
I scale the heavens, you are there!
I plunge to the depths, you are there!

If I fly toward the dawn,
or settle across the sea,
even there you take hold of me,
your right hand directs me.

If I think night will hide me
and darkness give me cover,
I find darkness is not dark.
For your night shines like day,
darkness and light are one. □

Search my heart, probe me, God!
Lead me along your ancient way.

You created every part of me,
knitting me in my mother's womb.
For such handiwork, I praise you.
Awesome this great wonder!
I see it so clearly!

You watched every bone
taking shape in secret,
forming in the hidden depths.
You saw my body grow
according to your design.

You recorded all my days
before they ever began.
How deep are your thoughts!
How vast their sum!
like countless grains of sand,
well beyond my grasp.

Lord, destroy the wicked,
save me from killers.
They plot evil schemes,
they blaspheme against you.

How I hate those who hate you!
How I detest those who defy you!
I hate with a deadly hate
these enemies of mine.

Search my heart, probe me, God!
Test and judge my thoughts.
Look! do I follow crooked paths?
Lead me along your ancient way. □

COLOSSIANS
1:12 – 20

Through Christ the universe was made,
things seen and unseen.

Give thanks to the Father,
who made us fit
for the holy community of light
and rescued us from darkness,
bringing us into the realm
of his beloved Son
who redeemed us,
forgiving our sins.

Christ is an image
of the God we cannot see.
Christ is firstborn in all creation.

Through Christ the universe was made,
things seen and unseen,
thrones, authorities, forces, powers.
Everything was created
through Christ and for Christ.

Before anything came to be, Christ was,
and the universe is held together by Christ.

Christ is also head of the body, the church,
its beginning as firstborn from the dead
to become in all things first.

For by God's good pleasure
Christ encompasses
the full measure of power,
reconciling creation with its source
and making peace by the blood of the cross. □

I acclaim the greatness of the Lord,
I delight in God my savior...

CANTICLE
OF MARY

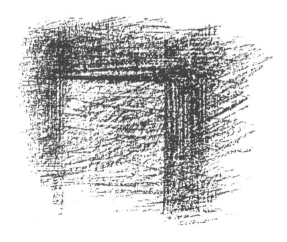

THURSDAY MORNING PRAYER

Let morning announce your love, my God,
for it is you I trust.

Hear me, faithful Lord!
bend to my prayer,
show compassion.
Do not judge me harshly;
in your sight, no one is just.

My enemy hunts me down,
grinding me to dust,
caging me with the dead
in lasting darkness.
My strength drains away,
my heart is numb.

I remember the ancient days,
I recall your wonders,
the work of your hands.
Dry as thirsty land,
I reach out for you.

Answer me quickly, Lord.
My strength is spent.
Do not hide from me
or I will fall into the grave.

Let morning announce your love,
for it is you I trust.
Show me the right way,
I offer you myself.

Rescue me from my foes,
you are my only refuge, Lord.
Teach me your will,
for you are my God.

Graciously lead me, Lord,
on to level ground.
I call on your just name,
keep me safe, free from danger.

In your great love for me,
disarm my enemies,
destroy their power,
for I belong to you. □

I will comfort you
as a mother nurses her child.

ISAIAH 66:
10 – 14a

Rejoice with Jerusalem!
Be glad for her,
all who love her.
Share her great joy,
all who know her sadness.

Now drink your fill
from her comforting breast,
enjoy her plentiful milk.

For this is what the Lord says:
"Look! to her I extend
peace like a river,
the wealth of the nations
like a stream in full flood.
And you will drink!

I will carry you on my shoulders,
cuddle you on my lap.
I will comfort you
as a mother nurses her child.

"Jerusalem will be your joy.
Your heart will rejoice to see it.
You will flourish like grass in spring." □

PSALM 147:
1 – 11

How good to sing God praise!
How lovely the sound!

How good to sing God praise!
How lovely the sound!

The Lord rebuilds Jerusalem
and gathers the exiles of Israel,
healing the brokenhearted,
binding their aching wounds.

God fixes the number of stars,
calling each by name.
Great is our God and powerful,
wise beyond all telling.
The Lord upholds the poor
but lets the wicked fall.

Sing thanks to the Lord,
sound the harp for our God.
The Lord stretches the clouds,
sending rain to the earth,
clothing mountains with green.

The Lord feeds the cattle
and young ravens when they call.
A horse's strength, a runner's speed —
they count for nothing!
The Lord favors the reverent,
those who trust in God's mercy. □

Praise the Lord, the God of Israel,
who shepherds the people and sets them free...

CANTICLE OF
ZECHARIAH

THURSDAY EVENING PRAYER

PSALM 144:
1 – 8

God, my love, my shield, my refuge,
you give me victory.

Praise God, God my rock
who trains my hands for battle,
my arms for war.

God, my love, my safety,
my stronghold and defender,
God, my shield, my refuge,
you give me victory.

Who are we that you care for us?
Why give a thought to mortals?
We are little more than breath;
our days, fleeting shadows.

Come, Lord, lower the heavens,
touch the mountains,
let them spew out smoke.
Strike lightning,
let your arrows fly,
scatter my enemies in terror.

Reach down from the heavens,
snatch me from crashing waves;
rescue me from strangers
who speak lies
and then swear to them. □

You bless us with great gifts, our God, our joy.

PSALM 144:
9 – 15

I sing you a <u>new</u> song, Lord,
I play my <u>ten</u>-stringed harp,
for you give vict<u>ory</u> to kings,
you rescue your s<u>er</u>vant, David.

Save me from the bitter sword,
deliver <u>me</u> from strangers,
who speak lies
and then <u>swear</u> to them.

God, you shape our sons
like tall, <u>stur</u>dy plants;
you sculpt our daughters
like pillars <u>for</u> a palace.

You fill our barns
with all <u>kinds</u> of food,
you bless our fields
with sheep by the thousands
and fatten <u>all</u> our cattle.

There is no breach <u>in</u> the walls,
no outcry in the <u>streets</u>, no exile.
We are a people blest <u>with</u> these gifts,
blest with the Lord <u>as</u> our God! □

Now is salvation,
the power and reign of God.

We thank you, Lord,
God and ruler of all,
who is and who was.
You have claimed your power
and begun to reign.

When the nations raged
your anger stirred.
Then was the moment
to judge the dead,
to reward your servants, the prophets,
to honor your holy ones
who honored your name,
small and great alike.

Now is salvation,
the power and reign of God;
the Christ holds command.
For the one who accused the saints
day and night before God
has now been driven out.

They won the battle
by the blood of the Lamb,
and by the power of their witness
despite the threat of death.
Citizens of heaven, rejoice. □

I acclaim the greatness of the Lord,
I delight in God my savior ...

CANTICLE
OF MARY

FRIDAY MORNING PRAYER

Creator, reshape my heart,
God, steady my spirit.

Have mercy, tender God,
forget that I defied you.
Wash away my sin,
cleanse me from my guilt.

I know my evil well,
it stares me in the face,
evil done to you alone
before your very eyes.

How right your condemnation!
Your verdict clearly just.
You see me for what I am,
a sinner before my birth.

You love those centered in truth;
teach me your hidden wisdom.
Wash me with fresh water,
wash me bright as snow.

Fill me with happy songs,
let the bones you bruised now dance.
Shut your eyes to my sin,
make my guilt disappear.

Creator, reshape my heart,
God, steady my spirit.
Do not cast me aside
stripped of your holy spirit.

Save me, bring back my joy,
support me, strengthen my will.
Then I will teach your way
and sinners will turn to you.

Help me, stop my tears,
and I will sing your goodness.
Lord, give me words
and I will shout your praise.

When I offer a holocaust,
the gift does not please you.
So I offer my shattered spirit;
a changed heart you welcome.

In your love make Zion lovely,
rebuild the walls of Jerusalem.
Then sacrifice will please you,
young bulls upon your altar. □

TOBIT 13:
8 – 11, 13 – 15

Celebrate, Jerusalem!
for all the just have gathered
to praise the living God.

Give witness to God's glory,
in Jerusalem give praise!

Jerusalem, holy city,
God punished you,
because your citizens did wrong.
Yet God will spare
the children of the just.

Make your praise worthy of God
who rules the ages,
that you may be a joyful city
where the temple rises again,
where God welcomes every exile
and loves for ever all who suffer.

A light shining over all the earth
will draw to your holy name
distant nations and peoples.
They will bring gifts
for the ruler of heaven.

All generations
will offer sacrifice here.
They will name you,
"Chosen Forever!"
Go now and celebrate
with the children of the just,
gathered to praise the living God.

Jerusalem, holy city,
blest are they who love you
and delight in your peace,
blest who mourn when you suffer.
They shall dance in your streets,
brimming over with joy.

Bless the Lord who reigns for ever. □

Praise the Lord with song, O Zion,
for God speaks to the earth
and the word speeds forth.

PSALM 147:
12 – 20

Jerusalem, give glory!
Praise God with song, O Zion!
For the Lord strengthens your gates
guarding your children within.
The Lord fills your land with peace,
giving you golden wheat.

God speaks to the earth,
the word speeds forth.
The Lord sends heavy snow
and scatters frost like ashes.

The Lord hurls chunks of hail.
Who can stand such cold?
God speaks, the ice melts;
God breathes, the streams flow.

God speaks his word to Jacob,
to Israel, his laws and decrees.
God has not done this for others,
no others receive this wisdom.

Hallelujah! □

CANTICLE OF
ZECHARIAH

Praise the Lord, the God of Israel,
who shepherds the people and sets them free...

FRIDAY EVENING PRAYER

I will bless you every day
and ponder your wonderful works.

PSALM 145:
1 – 13b

I will exalt you, God my king,
for ever bless your name.
I will bless you every day,
for ever praise your name.

Great is the Lord, highly to be praised,
great beyond our reach.

Age to age proclaims your works,
recounts your mighty deeds.
I ponder your splendor and glory
and all your wonderful works.

They reveal your fearful power,
I tell of your great deeds.
They recall your ample goodness,
joyfully sing your justice.

Gracious and merciful is the Lord,
slow to anger, full of love.
The Lord is good in every way,
merciful to every creature.

Let your works praise you, Lord,
your faithful ones bless you.
Let them proclaim your glorious reign,
let them tell of your might.

Let them make known to all
your might and glorious reign.
Your dominion lasts for ever,
your rule for all generations! □

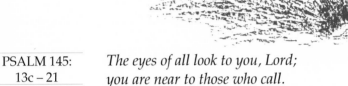

The eyes of all look to you, Lord;
you are near to those who call.

The Lord is faithful in every word
and gracious in every work.
The Lord supports the fallen,
raises those bowed down.

The eyes of all look to you,
you give them food in due time.
You open wide your hand
to feed all living things.

The Lord is just in every way,
loving in every deed.
The Lord is near to those who call,
who cry out from their hearts.

God grants them their desires,
hears their cry and saves them.
Those who love God are kept alive;
the wicked, the Lord destroys.

I will sing the Lord's praise,
let all flesh bless God's Name,
holy, both now and for ever. □

Your ways are right and true,
ruler of all nations.

REVELATION
15:3 – 4

All you do stirs wonder,
Lord, mighty God.
Your ways are right and true,
ruler of all nations.

Who would not be moved
to glorify your name?
For you alone are holy.

All nations will gather,
bowing low to you,
for your saving works
are plainly seen. □

I acclaim the greatness of the Lord,
I delight in God my Savior...

CANTICLE
OF MARY

PSALM 92

How good to thank you, Lord,
to sing your love at dawn.

How good to thank you, Lord,
to praise your name, Most High,
to sing your love at dawn,
your faithfulness at dusk
with sound of lyre and harp,
with music of the lute.
For your work brings delight,
your deeds invite song.

I marvel at what you do.
Lord, how deep your thought!
Fools do not grasp this,
nor the senseless understand.
Scoundrels spring up like grass,
flourish and quickly wither.
You, Lord, stand firm for ever.

See how your enemies perish,
scattered to the winds,
while you give me brute strength,
pouring rich oil upon me.
I have faced my enemies,
heard them plot against me.

The just grow tall like palm trees,
majestic like the cedars of Lebanon.
They are planted in the temple courts
and flourish in God's house,
green and heavy with fruit
even in old age.

Proclaim that God is just,
my rock without a fault. ☐

I will make you a new heart,
breathe new spirit into you.

EZEKIEL 36:
24 – 28

I will draw you from the nations,
gather you from exile
and bring you home.

I will wash you in fresh water,
rid you from the filth of idols
and make you clean again.

I will make you a new heart,
breathe new spirit into you.
I will remove your heart of stone,
give you back a heart of flesh.

I will give you my own spirit
to lead you in my ways,
faithful to what I command.

Then you will live in the land,
the land I gave your ancestors.
You will be my people
and I will be your God. ☐

Even the babble of infants
declares your strength, O God.

Lord our God,
the whole world tells
the greatness of your name.
Your glory reaches
beyond the stars.

Even the babble of infants
declares your strength,
your power to halt
the enemy and avenger.

I see your handiwork
in the heavens:
the moon and the stars
you set in place.

What is humankind
that you remember them,
the human race
that you care for them?

You treat them like gods,
dressing them in glory and splendor.
You give them charge of the earth,
laying all at their feet:

cattle and sheep,
wild beasts,
birds of the sky,
fish of the sea,
every swimming creature.

Lord our God,
the whole world tells
the greatness of your name. □

Praise the Lord, the God of Israel,
who shepherds the people and sets them free...

CANTICLE OF
ZECHARIAH

MIDDAY PRAYER

PSALM 23

The Lord is my shepherd,
I need nothing more.
You give me rest in green meadows,
setting me near calm waters,
where you revive my spirit.

You guide me along sure paths,
you are true to your name.
Though I should walk in death's dark valley,
I fear no evil with you by my side,
your shepherd's staff to comfort me.

You spread a table before me
as my foes look on.
You soothe my head with oil;
my cup is more than full.

Goodness and love will tend me
every day of my life.
I will dwell in the house of the Lord
as long as I shall live. □

PSALM 25

Lord, I give myself to you.

I trust you, God;
do not fail me,
nor let my enemies gloat.
No one loyal is shamed,
but traitors know disgrace.

Teach me how to live,
Lord, show me the way.
Steer me toward your truth,
you, my saving God,
you, my constant hope.

Recall your tenderness,
your lasting love.
Remember me, not my faults,
the sins of my youth.
To show your own goodness,
God, remember me.

Good and just is the Lord,
guiding those who stray.
God leads the poor,
pointing out the path.

God's ways are faithful love
for those who keep the covenant.
Be true to your name, O Lord,
forgive my sin, though great.

Do you respect God?
Then God will guide your choice.
Your life will be full,
your heirs will keep the land.
God befriends the faithful
teaches them the covenant.

I keep looking to God
to spring me from this trap.
Turn, treat me as your friend,
I am empty and poor.

Release my trapped heart,
free me from my anguish.
See my misery, my pain,
take my sins away.

See how they mob me,
this crowd that hates me.
Protect me and save my life.
Keep me from disgrace,
for I take shelter in you.
Let integrity stand guard
as I wait for you.

Free Israel, O God,
from all its troubles. □

PSALM 34

I will never stop thanking God,
with constant words of praise.
My soul will boast of God;
the poor will hear me and be glad.

Join me in praising the Lord,
together tell of God's name.
I asked and the Lord responded,
freed me from all my fears.

Turn to God, be bright with joy;
you shall never be let down.
I begged and God heard,
took my burdens from me.

God's angel defends the faithful,
guards them on every side.
Drink in the richness of God,
enjoy the strength of the Lord.

Live in awe of God, you saints:
you will want for nothing.
Even if lions go hungry,
those seeking God are fed.

Come to me, children, listen:
learn to cherish the Lord.
Do you long for life,
for time to enjoy success?

Keep your tongue from evil,
keep lies far from your lips.
Shun evil, go after good,
press on, seek after peace.

God confronts the wicked
to blot them out for ever,
but turns toward the just
to hear their cry for help.

The troubled call out; God hears,
saves them from all distress.
God stays near broken hearts,
heals the wounded spirit.

The good endure great trials,
but God comes to their rescue
and guards their every bone
so not one is broken.

Evil kills its own kind,
dooms the wicked to death.
God saves those who keep faith;
no trusting soul is doomed. ▢

PSALM 71

Lord, you are my shelter,
do not fail me.
You always do right;
deliver me, rescue me,
hear me and save me.

Be my rock and haven,
to whom I can always turn;
be my tower of strength,
keep me safe.
The ruthless and wicked trap me;
reach out to free me.

You are my hope, O Lord,
from the days of my youth.
I have relied on you since birth,
my strength from my mother's womb;
I will praise you always.

I am shunned like the plague,
but you keep me in your care.
I am filled with your praises,
all day I sing your glory.
Now I am old, my strength fails,
do not toss me aside.

My enemies scheme against me,
they have designs on my life.
They think God has left me.
"Strike," they say, "no one will help."

Do not hold back, Lord,
run to my rescue.
Disgrace my accusers,
wrap them in shame,
make my enemies
face utter ruin.

I will not lose hope,
never stop praising you.
My lips speak your goodness,
praise each day your saving acts,
though I cannot count them all.
I will enter your palace proclaiming,
"Lord God, you alone are just."

From childhood till now
you taught me to praise your wonders.
Do not leave me, Lord,
now that I am old.

I can still recount
to a new generation
your power and strength.
Your goodness is boundless,
your works so great;
who can equal you?

You wrack me with torment,
but you give back my life
and raise me from this grave.
You will restore my honor
and wrap me again in mercy.

I will thank you, Lord,
for your true friendship
and play the lyre and harp for you,
to the Holy One of Israel.
I will sing out with joy,
sing of how you saved me.

From morning till night
I will trumpet your goodness;
those who sought my ruin
are defeated and shamed. □

Hear my prayer, Lord,
let my cry reach you.
Do not turn from me
in my hour of need.
When I call, listen,
answer me at once.

For my days dissolve like smoke,
my bones are burned to ash.
My heart withers away like grass.
I even forget to eat,
so consumed am I with grief.
My skin hangs on my bones.

Like a gull lost in the desert,
like an owl haunting the ruins,
I keep a solitary watch,
a lone bird on a roof.
All day my enemies mock me,
they make my name a curse.

For bread, I eat ashes,
tears salt my drink.
You lifted me up in anger
and threw me to the ground.
My days pass into evening,
I wither like the grass.

But you, Lord, preside for ever,
every age remembers you.
Rise with mercy for Zion,
for now is the time for pity.
Your servants treasure every stone,
they cherish even the rubble.

Nations will fear your name,
your glory will humble kings.
When you rebuild Zion's walls,
you will appear in glory, Lord.
You hear the homeless pleading
and do not mock their prayer.

Write this down for those to come,
a people created to praise our God:
"The Lord watches from on high,
searches the earth from heaven.

"God hears the prisoner's groan
and sets the doomed free
to sing the Lord's name in Zion,
God's praise in Jerusalem.
There the nations and peoples
gather to serve the Lord."

God has broken me in my prime,
has cut short my days.
I say: "My God, do not take me.
My life is only half-spent,
while you live from age to age."

Long ago you made the earth,
the heavens, too, are your work.
Should they decay, you remain.
Should they wear out like a robe,
like clothing changed and thrown away,
you are still the same.
Your years will never end.

May your servants' line last for ever,
our children grow strong before you. □

I will bless you, Lord my God!

You fill the world with awe.
You dress yourself in light,
in rich, majestic light.

You stretched the sky like a tent,
built your house beyond the rain.
You ride upon the clouds,
the wind becomes your wings,
the storm becomes your herald,
your servants, bolts of light.

You made the earth solid,
fixed it for good.
You made the sea a cloak,
covering hills and all.

At your command
the sea fled your thunder,
swept over mountains,
down the valleys to its place.
You set its limits,
never to drown the earth again.

You feed springs that feed brooks,
rushing down ravines,
water for wild beasts,
for wild asses to drink.
Birds nest nearby
and sing among the leaves.

You drench the hills
with rain from high heaven.
You nourish the earth
with what you create.

You make grass grow for cattle,
make plants grow for people,
food to eat from the earth
and wine to warm the heart,
oil to glisten on faces
and bread for bodily strength.

In Lebanon God planted trees,
the flourishing cedar.
Sparrows nest in the branches,
the stork in treetops.
High crags for wild goats,
rock holes for badgers.

Your moon knows when to rise,
your sun when to set.
Your darkness brings on night
when wild beasts prowl.
The young lions roar to you
in search of prey.

They slink off to dens
to rest at daybreak,
then people rise to work
until the daylight fades.

God, how fertile your genius!
You shape each thing,
you fill the world
with what you do.

I watch the sea, wide and deep,
filled with fish, large and small,
with ships that ply their trade,
and your own toy, Leviathan.

All look to you for food
when they hunger;
you provide it and they feed.
You open your hand, they feast;
you turn away, they fear.

You steal their breath,
they drop back into dust.
Breathe into them, they rise;
the face of the earth comes alive!

Let God's glory endure
and the Lord delight in creating.
One look from God, earth quivers;
one touch, and mountains erupt.

I will sing to my God,
make music for the Lord
as long as I live.
Let my song give joy to God
who is a joy to me.
Rid the world of sinners,
rid it of evil!

I will bless you, Lord!
Hallelujah! □

PSALM 128

How good to revere the Lord,
to walk in God's path.

Your table rich from labor —
how good for you!
Your beloved, a fruitful vine
in the warmth of your home.

Like olive shoots,
children surround your table.
This is your blessing
when you revere the Lord.

May the Lord bless you from Zion!
May you see Jerusalem prosper
every day of your life.
May you see your children's children,
and on Israel, peace! □

NIGHT PRAYER

PSALM 4

Answer when I call, faithful God.
You cleared away my trouble;
be good to me, listen to my prayer.

How long, proud fools,
will you insult my honor,
loving lies and chasing shadows?
Look! God astounds believers,
the Lord listens when I call.

Tremble, but do not despair.
Attend to your heart,
be calm through the night,
worship with integrity,
trust in the Lord.

Cynics ask, "Who will bless us?
Even God has turned away."
You give my heart more joy
than all their grain and wine.
I sleep secure at night,
you keep me in your care. □

PSALM 31

Shelter me, Lord,
save me from shame.
Let there be justice:
save me!

Help me! Listen!
Be quick to the rescue!
Be my fortress, my refuge.

You, my rock and fortress,
prove your good name.
Guide me, lead me,
free me from their trap.

You are my shelter;
I put myself in your hands,
knowing you will save me,
Lord God of truth.

You hate the slaves of idols,
but I trust in you.
I dance for joy at your constant love.

You saw me suffer,
you know my pain.
You let no enemy cage me,
but set my feet on open ground.

Pity me, Lord,
I hurt all over;
my eyes are swollen,
my heart and body ache.

Grief consumes my life,
sighs fill my days;
guilt saps my strength,
my bones dissolve.

Enemies mock me,
make me the butt of jokes.
Neighbors scorn me,
strangers avoid me.
Forgotten like the dead,
I am a shattered jar.

I hear the crowd whisper,
"Attack on every side!"
as they scheme to take my life.

But I trust in you, Lord.
I say, "You are my God,
My life is in your hands."
Snatch me from the enemy,
ruthless in their chase.

Look on me with love,
save your servant.
I call on you;
save me from shame!

Shame the guilty,
silence them with the grave.
Silence the lips that lie,
that scorn the just.

How rich your goodness
to those who revere you!
The whole world can see:
whoever seeks your help
finds how lavish you are.

You are shelter from gossips,
a place to hide from busy tongues.
Blessed be the Lord!
God's love encircles me
like a protecting wall.

I said too quickly,
"God has cut me off!"
But you heard my cry
when I prayed for help.

Love the Lord, all faithful people,
the Lord your guardian,
who fully repays the proud.
Be strong, be brave,
all who wait for God. □

Save me, Lord my God!
By day, by night, I cry out.
Let my prayer reach you;
turn, listen to me.

I am steeped in trouble,
ready for the grave.
I am like one destined for the pit,
a warrior deprived of strength,
forgotten among the dead,
buried with the slaughtered
for whom you care no more.

PSALM 88

You tossed me to the bottom of the pit,
into its murky darkness,
your anger pulled me down
like roaring waves.

You took my friends away,
disgraced me before them.
Trapped here with no escape,
I cannot see beyond my pain.

Lord, I cry out to you all day,
my hands keep reaching out.
Do you work marvels for the dead?
Can shadows rise and sing praise?

Is your mercy sung in the grave,
your lasting love in Sheol?
Are your wonders known in the pit,
your justice, in forgotten places?

But I cry out to you, God,
each morning I plead with you.
Why do you reject me, Lord?
Why do you hide your face?

Weak since childhood,
I am often close to death.
Your torments track me down,
your rage consumes me,
your trials destroy me.

All day, they flood around me,
pressing down, closing me in.
You took my friends from me,
darkness is all I have left. □

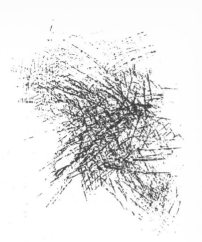

All you sheltered by the Most High,
who live in Almighty God's shadow,
say to the Lord, "My refuge, my fortress,
my God in whom I trust!"

God will free you from hunters' snares,
will save you from deadly plague,
will cover you like a nesting bird.
God's wings will shelter you.

No nighttime terror shall you fear,
no arrows shot by day,
no plague that prowls the dark,
no wasting scourge at noon.

A thousand may fall at your side,
ten thousand at your right hand.
But you shall live unharmed:
God is sturdy armor.

You have only to open your eyes
to see how the wicked are repaid.
You have the Lord as refuge,
have made the Most High your stronghold.

PSALM 91

No evil shall ever touch you,
no harm come near your home.
God instructs angels
to guard you wherever you go.

With their hands they support you,
so your foot will not strike a stone.
You will tread on lion and viper,
trample tawny lion and dragon.

"I deliver all who cling to me,
raise the ones who know my name,
answer those who call me,
stand with those in trouble.
These I rescue and honor,
satisfy with long life,
and show my power to save." □

PSALM 103

My soul, bless the Lord,
bless God's holy name!
My soul, bless the Lord,
hold dear all God's gifts!

Bless God, who forgives your sin
and heals every illness,
who snatches you from death
and enfolds you with tender care,
who fills your life with richness
and gives you an eagle's strength.

The Lord, who works justice
and defends the oppressed,
teaches Moses and Israel
divine ways and deeds.

The Lord is tender and caring,
slow to anger, rich in love.
God will not accuse us long,
nor bring our sins to trial,
nor exact from us in kind
what our sins deserve.

As high as heaven above earth,
so great is God's love for believers.
As far as east from west,
so God removes our sins.

As tender as father to child,
so gentle is God to believers.
The Lord knows how we are made,
remembers we are dust.

Our days pass by like grass,
our prime like a flower in bloom.
A wind comes, the flower goes,
empty now its place.

God's love is from all ages,
God's justice beyond all time
for believers of each generation:
those who keep the covenant,
who take care to live the law.

The Lord reigns from heaven,
rules over all there is.
Bless the Lord, you angels,
strong and quick to obey,
attending to God's word.

Bless the Lord, you powers,
eager to serve God's will.
Bless the Lord, you creatures,
everywhere under God's rule.
My soul, bless the Lord! □

PSALM 134

Bless the Lord,
all who serve in God's house,
who stand watch
throughout the night.

Lift up your hands
in the holy place
and bless the Lord.

And may God,
the maker of earth and sky,
bless you from Zion. □

Lord, let your servant
now die in peace,
for you kept your promise.

With my own eyes
I see the salvation
you prepared for all peoples:

a light of revelation for the Gentiles
and glory to your people Israel. □

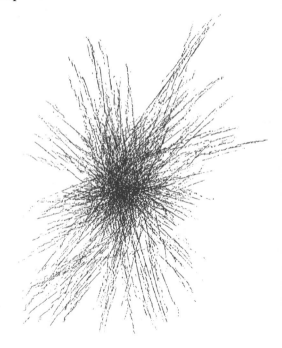

INVITATORY AND
GOSPEL CANTICLES

INVITATORY

Come, sing with joy to God,
shout to our savior, our rock.
Enter God's presence with praise,
enter with shouting and song.

A great God is the Lord,
over the gods like a king.
God cradles the depths of the earth,
holds fast the mountain peaks.
God shaped the ocean and owns it,
formed the earth by hand.

Come, bow down and worship,
kneel to the Lord our maker.
This is our God, our shepherd,
we are the flock led with care.

Listen today to God's voice:
"Harden no heart as at Meribah,
on that day in the desert at Massah.
There your people tried me,
though they had seen my work.

"Forty years with that lot!
I said: They are perverse,
they do not accept my ways.
So I swore in my anger:
They shall not enter my rest." □

GOSPEL CANTICLES AND ANTIPHONS

Protect us, Lord, as we stay awake;
watch over us as we sleep,
that, awake, we may keep watch with Christ,
and, asleep, rest in his peace.

Lord, let your servant
now die in peace,
for you kept your promise.

With my own eyes
I see the salvation
you prepared for all peoples:

a light of revelation for the Gentiles
and glory to your people Israel. □

Ordinary Time

Praise the Lord, the God of Israel.

Out of God's deepest mercy
a dawn will come from on high,
light for those shadowed by death.

Lord, guide our feet on the way to peace.

Advent

Take courage!
The Lord our God comes to save us.

Christmas

Glory to God in the highest,
and peace to God's people on earth, alleluia.

Lent

If you wish to be my disciple,
deny yourself, take up your cross, and follow me.

Easter

Thanks be to God who has given us victory
through our Lord Jesus Christ, alleluia.

Praise the Lord, the God of Israel,
who shepherds the people and sets them free.

God raises from David's house
a child with power to save.
Through the holy prophets
God promised in ages past
to save us from enemy hands,
from the grip of all who hate us.

The Lord favored our ancestors
recalling the sacred covenant,
the pledge to our ancestor Abraham,
to free us from our enemies,
so we might worship without fear
and be holy and just all our days.

And you, child, will be called
Prophet of the Most High,
for you will come to prepare
a pathway for the Lord
by teaching the people salvation
through forgiveness of their sin.

Out of God's deepest mercy
a dawn will come from on high,
light for those shadowed by death,
a guide for our feet on the way to peace. □

Ordinary Time

I acclaim the greatness of the Lord,
I delight in God my savior.

The mighty arm of God
scatters the proud and raises up the humble.

God, wonderful in power,
has used that strength for me.

Advent

Come to us, Lord,
come with peace to save your people.

Christmas

Let us dance with delight in the Lord,
our hearts filled with rejoicing,
for eternal salvation has appeared on the earth,
alleluia.

Lent

Drink the water the Lord shall give,
and never be thirsty again.

Easter

Stay with us, Lord,
for evening draws near and daylight is fading,
alleluia.

I acclaim the greatness of the Lord,
I delight in God my savior,
who regarded my humble state.
Truly from this day on
all ages will call me blest.

For God, wonderful in power,
has used that strength for me.
Holy the name of the Lord!
whose mercy embraces the faithful,
one generation to the next.

The mighty arm of God
scatters the proud in their conceit,
pulls tyrants from their thrones,
and raises up the humble.
The Lord fills the starving
and lets the rich go hungry.

God rescues lowly Israel,
recalling the promise of mercy,
the promise made to our ancestors,
to Abraham's heirs for ever. □

The Design

In preparing this book, I have tried to stand with those who have beautifully inscribed and illustrated the words of the psalms through centuries. I thought of the rhythms of daily life and the cycle of seasons and strove for a design that would be seen over and over yet would invite fresh sight every day, a design that would exalt the words and provide functional elements that would disappear unless the reader is looking for them.

All involved in this book have spent much, much time attending to every detail of its production. The typeface is Palatino, a popular old style face designed by Hermann Zapf in 1950. The typesetting for the body of the book was done by Phyllis Martinez. Kari Nicholls typeset the front matter. These pages were printed by Congress Printing Company, Chicago, Illinois, on 70# Cream St. Lawrence Matte. Case-bound editions were bound at Zonne Bookbinders, Inc., of Chicago.

Kerry Perlmutter

The Art

Through centuries artists have illuminated the pages of the psalms. This ancient poetry is still so pertinent that contemporary visual expression must interpret and be interpreted by the tradition, thereby honoring the eyes and voices praying these words today.

The psalms offer such richness of imagery. By working abstractly and through elimination, I sought a residue of essence that would hint at the content. Inspired by words of beauty and praise, lament and pain, I wanted to express with genuine marks in the spaces around these words the depth and variety of emotions evident in the psalms.

For me, drawing is the most straightforward and unpretentious method, and I made drawing after drawing on paper placed over various textured surfaces. This is called "frottage" or rubbing technique. The result fragments the solid shapes, giving them a less defined quality. I was struck by movement and the varied sense of energy and rhythm found throughout the poems; I wanted to echo this with a gestural quality in the drawings. Reproduction of the once black images in copper ink gives a more ephemeral quality; what seems a random scattering of the drawings is for the most part intuitive, yet hints that these words cannot be contained or framed in predictable ways. Throughout the making of this art I kept in mind that our eyes must first and last be centered on the words of these pages, with the illuminations a part of our peripheral vision as we pray.

Linda Ekstrom